THE POETICAL WORKS OF A. B. TODD

F. W. Todd

THE POETICAL WORKS

OF

A. B. TODD

WITH

AUTOBIOGRAPHY

AND

PORTRAIT

"I have considered the days of old."—PSALM lxxvii. 5.

" From me I must not, may not say,
　What these long years have borne away,
　What ardent toils they have made void,
　What harvests of rich hope destroyed ;
　What blooms immortal they have shorn,
　What tender ties most rudely torn
　Were long to tell, both sad and true
　Yet neither rare, alas ! nor new."—JOHN STRUTHERS.

OLIPHANT, ANDERSON, & FERRIER
EDINBURGH AND LONDON
1906

DAVID M'COWAN, Esq.

Dear Mr M'Cowan,

I dedicate to you the following autobiography, giving an account of my long, chequered, and busy life and literary aspirations, with, also, the new edition of the poems written by me over the long period of sixty years. And I do so not merely because you are a native of, and have done honour to the district in which I have had my home from early manhood to old age; but because that not only in Cumnock, but in the great city of Glasgow, and throughout the West of Scotland, your name has long been synonymous with all that is pure in life, noble in purpose, and generous in action; and also because that success in life has not made you, even once, forget the home and the home affections of your youth; or that—

> " There's a Divinity that shapes our ends,
> Rough hew them as we will ";

and because the moral progress of the human race, and more than all, the progress of the Kingdom of Christ in the world— have ever been dear to your heart, and have always had your unstinted support. And I express not only my own earnest wish, but that also of all who know you, that you may be long spared to aid in promoting these great ends in the world, and to practise that virtue which you learned so early in life, "the luxury of doing good"; and that now, at the sunset of life, you may have not only bodily health, but that inward "Peace of God which passeth all understanding," and

> " That an old age serene and bright,
> And lovely as a Lapland night,
> Shall lead thee to thy grave."

Permit me then, here and ever, to subscribe myself,

Most truly and affectionately,

Your obedient servant,

A. B. TODD.

PREFACE

IT is, I believe, a very general experience that when we grow old we, mentally, live far more in the past than in the future. We then cease, in a great measure, to look ahead—for the present life at least—which, then, is bounded by a very near horizon; and the scenes and events which the imagination may picture as still lying in front of us then begin to get far less alluring. Not so, however, with those which lie behind us; for in spite of both experience and philosophy the scenes and events of the far distant past, and especially those of our childhood, seem to us, now, to have had a glamour and a glitter about and around them which, in reality, they never possessed; though, looked back upon now—when standing upon the threshold of another world—they seem to have been full of delights almost beyond conception or expression, and on which, now that they are gone, the mind loves to luxuriate and dwell, and which, even as the years go gliding by on the ever-moving wings of time, we care not to attempt to shake off; and I, at least, have not been able to do so,

> " But feel it pleasant to rehearse
> The scenes of youth in prose or verse,
> To live again my young days over,
> To be once more the youthful lover—
> A pensive pleasure mixed with pain,
> For, ah! we ne'er grow young again."

It may be that others will take an interest in, and read with some degree of pleasure, the reminiscences of one who all his life, and even yet, at the age of fourscore and four years, has had deep and strong poetic feelings and sympathies ; one who has been intoxicated with the beauties of nature, and who has written much both in poetry and prose ; who has reached his diamond jubilee as an author —having published a volume of poems in 1846—and who has been a journalist for the long period of sixty-two years. If the reader receives but half the pleasure from the perusal of the following pages that I have had in writing them— particularly the autobiographic portion of the volume—then this circumstance will add greatly to my own pleasure, and the volume will not have been written and published in vain.

A. B. TODD.

CONTENTS

MISCELLANEOUS POEMS

CONTENTS

REMINISCENCES OF A LONG LIFE

CHAPTER I

BIRTH AND PARENTAGE

" O Life, how sweet thy dawning morn,
The heart's warm channels all unworn,
All objects fresh, all nature new,
And all the world imagin'd true !
Why is it man and woman's fate,
To find thee out a monstrous cheat ?
Yet, in fond hope, to grasp thee fast,
A sad illusion to the last."

JOHN STRUTHERS.

BORN on 6th February 1822, I am now, therefore—as years go—an old man, and in the now more than fourscore years of a busy life, manual and literary, I have seen many changes, and met and had communication with some men of note ; and having from a very early age been much given to observation, to take notice of the changes of beliefs, of fashions, customs, and national progress ; besides, amid my other avocations, having now been a regular writer for the newspaper press for more than sixty years, during half of which time I have had charge of, and written largely for, *The Cumnock Express*, I have been frequently urged to write an account of some of the most outstanding events of my life, and to do so in the form of an Autobiography. This, trusting to a memory better and more retentive than, perhaps, the generality of men, and to a very large mass of correspondence, I now essay to do.

Mauchline (made famous in pre-Reformation times by the monks of Melrose planting a colony there, then by the preaching of Wishart and Knox, by the Covenanters, and latterly by Robert Burns), is the parish of my birth, and Craighall—about two and a half miles north of the town of Mauchline—is the place where I first saw the light. The place, locally known by the name of Backhill, was then a little farm, but long ago it was laid into, and now forms part of the larger one of Boghead. To Craighall my father entered at Whitsunday, 1795, and there his eldest son was born two months before the death of Robert Burns (whom my father knew), and there his whole family of eight sons and seven daughters were born, I being his seventh son and fourteenth child; and that they were sprung from a healthy stock may be inferred from the fact that the youngest of them was over twenty-one years of age before there was a death in the family. The mother of the first ten, however, having died, my father married a second time, some two years after her death.

Craighall with a northern exposure, has an extensive and a pleasant prospect to the north and north-west. The soil was naturally poor, with the exception of a rich and productive meadow, lying between it and the Hill of Burneight, and which, in the long ago, had evidently been a loch of considerable size. Immediately in front of the house was one of those wide, deep, and dangerous wells once so common about most country houses. It was cradled, or built round the sides with rough stones, having steps leading down to the water, and because of an accident which happened to my mother there, only one week before I was born, I had nearly never seen the light. In stooping to take water from the well, one of the stone steps slid away, and she fell headforemost into the well, and sank to the bottom of it. Fortunately for her, the well was sufficiently wide to allow her to turn, which she did, and rose to the surface and got hold of an osier which grew at its mouth. She succeeded in getting her foot on one of the other steps, and so managed to get out, and thus narrowly escaped drowning, else she and I would then have gone to " the land of silence and the shadow of death " together.

My mother, Mary Gibb, was the daughter of James Gibb of Auchmillan, in the parish of Mauchline, one of whose ancestors—according to the Chartulary of Melrose—received the lands from the monks, the charter being dated 20th February 1555. One of a large family, my mother was born in August 1779, just twenty years and seven months after Robert Burns, whom she quite well remembered having seen. An ardent lover of Nature and of ballad lore herself, she early fostered mine. At her lap, when a very little child, I listened—and listening, often wept—as she repeated from memory many of the best and most pathetic ballads of our native land; or she would sing to me in a voice of witching sweetness, " The Soldier's Return " of Burns, or "The Wounded Hussar " of Campbell ; and whatever literary tastes I have I very much owe to her, and even yet her words of wisdom and her gentle, winning, Christian ways greatly influence my life ; while I almost feel as if her spirit—for more than thirty years now in the better land—was daily luring me onward to the Beulah which is above. When but little more than an infant she taught me to " consider the lilies of the field " ; and to her pure and elevated tastes and dear, delightful lessons, I owe that deep and lasting pleasure which I have always derived from a contemplation of the waving woods, the wimpling streams, the blue or purple-coloured hills, the green, daisy-covered lea, and

" The immortal lights that live along the sky."

Most assiduously did she instruct me in these two best of books—the book of Nature and our grand old English Bible. Once when reading with her the lives of the ancient Patriarchs of Palestine I lamented that never, in all likelihood, would I be able to visit those plains where they had pastured their sheep, or those hills from which they had looked down upon " the great sea," and where they had pitched their tents and built their altars—the land, too, which had become hallowed ground from having been trod by the footsteps of " the Son of the Highest " during the days of His humiliation—she surprised me by saying that though I might never be able to visit the Holy Land, I yet might every day gaze upon one glorious object upon which all the Patriarchs' eyes had rested; and she bade me look away to the setting sun which just then was sending up its rings of welling light from the west and flooding the splintered peaks of Arran with an inexpressible glory and beauty, and said, "There, see! on that same sun the Patriarch Job must have looked from the Arabian sands; Moses from the summit of Sinai; David, when a shepherd boy, from the plains of Bethlehem; and the Saviour from the green top of Mount Tabor and from the western slopes of Olivet"; and though this was a matter which no one would dispute, yet it struck me as strange that I had never thought of it before.

In the Bible she greatly delighted, and with its pages she was most familiar, and she soon made me tolerably so also. Its pages were the first I had ever seen traced by her soft intelligent eyes, and from that "book divine" I read to her words of promise, hope, and comfort, when the final scene came. They were the last words which ever fell upon her ear on earth. These—the 34th Psalm, and the 14th chapter of St John's Gospel, which, at her own request, I read to her on the last day of her life—I have ever delighted more in since than in any other portions of the sacred volume. To her I owe very much of what knowledge I possess, and any literary power, culture, and poetic leanings and skill which I have. No language of mine can express how greatly I love and revere her memory, and though more than forty years have glided by on the unstaying wings of Time since, at the age of more than fourscore years, she calmly took her departure for the better and the brighter land, and now my once raven locks are waxing thin and bare, ever since then I have had less sunshine in my life than before, and even at this distant day, when taking my solitary walks by wood and waterfall, the tears of loved remembrance will occasionally come into my eyes as I call up into my memory the looks and the words of that best of mothers, and the holy, happy fireside scenes of a long and fast receding past. In "The Circling Year," I have embalmed her memory in the poem on "August," of which these are the closing lines :—

" With radiant countenance she pass'd away,
 That left behind was only breathless clay.
 Fast fell our tears, but for ourselves they flow'd,
 And her lov'd guidance on life's perilous road;
 Her wise words spoken, and her cheering smile,
 Her winning, gentle ways, all free from guile.
 The light which ever lighten'd her own way,
 Show'd us the right when lured to step astray.
 We leave thee, Mother, in the Saviour's smile,
 And hope to meet thee in some after while.
 O for thy faith, and hope, and holy will;
 Thy brave, large heart, under each worldly ill;
 That we may go, life's constant battle by,
 To join thee waiting for us in the sky."

O, mothers, mothers! if you could only know how great and all-important is the influence which you exercise on the young minds of your little ones, how careful would you be in all you teach them, or say or do before them, and how greatly would you exert yourselves to form their minds aright, by instilling into them that knowledge alone which is pure, good, and useful. The seed you sow in their young minds now is destined to yield immortal fruit, and this will yet be seen by yourselves to be the case when you look back upon this state of high probation through the mellow light of a far, future eternity.

My father was pious, honest, and industrious. He knew little about, and cared nothing for, literary culture; but in the history of the great and protracted Covenanting struggle of the seventeenth century, and in all the writings bearing upon that period, and the events which then took place, he was deeply read and perfectly versed. He knew every page of " The Hind Let Loose," " The Cloud of Witnesses," " The Scots Worthies," Crookshank's " History of the Sufferings of the Church of Scotland from the Restoration till the Revolution," and other works of the period. The most prominent " Hillmen " of that time— Cargill, Cameron, Blackadder, Peden, Renwick, and others—were the heroes of the Covenant whom he greatly admired and revered. Fenwick—of which parish he was a native—because of its many Covenanting memories, and

B

John Howie of Lochgoin, author of " The Scots Worthies," whom he knew well and with whom he had worshipped in the old Cameronian Church at Crookedholm, was to him " the holy land." Beyond a doubt, had he lived during the evil days of the last Persecution he would have fought with Hamilton and Burley at Drumclog and with Hackstone and Cameron at Airsmoss, and because of his lofty courage, great strength, and long brawny arm would have dealt death among the savage troopers, and might, not unlikely, have succeeded in sending the ferocious Claverhouse himself to his long home among the marshes of Drumclog in the hour of his defeat, instead of his being left to die with the dubious fame of Killiecrankie (which battle was won by mere accident and not by generalship at all) clinging to his black, bloated, and bloody memory.

Although an out-and-out Covenanter, my father was no fanatic like Balfour of Burley and perhaps a few others, but a calm and sober thinker, well read in his Bible (no portion or page of which he doubted in the least was written by Divine inspiration), in the early fathers of the Church, in the Puritan divines, and in the religious litera-ture of his own day. His piety, however, was of a less cheerful kind than that of my mother, and he was rather wanting in that gentle and kindly charity which peculiarly characterised hers ; and she did much to soften down and gently to rub off the more hard and knotty points from his beliefs and creed. He died in December, 1850, eleven years before my mother—she being just that number of years younger—and like her, he was in his eighty-third year at the time of his death. For the previous three years he, with my mother, resided with me at Wellhill Tileworks, in the parish of New Cumnock, of which I was then tacksman, and just before he took his last illness, which was only of a month's duration, there occurred one of those occasional and utterly inexplicable circumstances, which may be denied, but can never be explained by either science or philosophy. Somehow, my father had never been in the habit of addressing my mother by her Christian name. He either addressed her as " gudewife," or spoke to her without giving her any name at all. One morning, just after breakfast, about the middle of the month of November—when he was quite in his usual health—my mother left him sitting in his arm-chair reading, while she went into another apartment to tidy it up, and while engaged in doing so she was startled by hearing him call out to her in a sharp, clear and rather loud voice, " Are you there, Mary ? " when she hurried to him with all the speed she could and found him still reading and in the same attitude in which she had left him shortly before. Anxiously inquiring what it was for which he had called her, he assured her that he had not spoken, that he had neither called her nor had he been even reading aloud. She spoke to me about the strange circumstance a few hours after, and though perplexed by it, we were beginning to think little more of it, when, just two days after, my father fell ill and his perpetual cry whenever my mother was out of his presence was—" Are you there, Mary ? "—which he kept on doing till the end came, or until within two days of his death, when he ceased to speak or to recognise any one. No sooner had he become ill and commenced to call her by name than with great composure, but with a solemn sadness of countenance, my mother took me aside and told me, quite confidently, that he would not recover, for that cry of his was the very one she had heard the two days before when he was well, and when he assured her he had not opened his lips.

Good and pious man though he was, and with his firm trust on the " Rock of Ages," he had, nevertheless, all throughout his long life had such a great fear of death and horror of the grave as greatly distressed us all ; but from the day he took his last illness, although his mind was clear and unclouded till within two days of the end, all fear of death entirely left him and he dreaded the grave no more than his bed. On the night of his death I was sitting by his bedside, while my mother was in the byre milking the single cow we kept there. For two whole days and nights he had lain with his eyes closed, and though breathing calmly had not spoken a word, and seemed unconscious to all around him, when to my great surprise he lifted up his right hand and in a firm, clear voice repeated these first sixteen lines of the 46th Psalm, and which, because of their abiding interest to me—their own sublimity, and the confident hope which they are so well calculated to inspire in the mind of every Christian —I cannot help giving here; the more so, too, as it has become very much the fashion to underrate the Psalms, and to make light of our metrical version, though, with here and there a rugged and unmusical line, it contains the loftiest and noblest poetry ever penned, being at the same time so literal; nor are the following lines, with which, quivering upon his lips, my father went down—fearing no evil—into " The swellings of Jordan," excelled by any for their lofty grandeur :

> " God is our refuge and our strength,
>   In straits a present aid ;
> Therefore, although the earth remove,
>   We will not be afraid.
> Though hills amidst the seas be cast,
>   Though waters roaring make,
> And troubled be ; yea though the hills
>   By swelling seas do shake.

> " A river is whose streams do glad
>   The city of our God ;
> The holy place wherein the Lord
>   Most high hath His abode.
> God in the midst of her doth dwell,
>   Nothing shall her remove ;
> The Lord to her an helper will,
>   And that right early prove."

He ceased, his hand fell, and though he opened his eyes I instantly saw that he was passing away, and I had barely time to call my mother before the spirit of the aged pilgrim had returned to God who gave it. In the poem on December, in my " Circling Year," I have thus referred to the event—

" 'Tis long since then, and now my locks are grey;
 He first I saw enter death's gloomy vale,
But many since that dull December day
 I've seen descend, 'mid many an anguish wail.

" The road seems lonely, since we go alone
 On our dark voyage to the unseen shore;
O! for the guidance of the Holy One,
 To light the way, and quell the billows' roar."

CHAPTER II

EARLY RECOLLECTIONS AND SCHOOL DAYS

"When weary wi' toil, or when canker'd wi' care,
  Remembrance takes wing like a bird o' the air,
  And, free as a thought that ye canna confine,
  It flees to the pleasures o' bonnie lang syne.
  In fancy I bound o'er the green sunny braes
  And drink up the bliss o' the lang summer days,
  Or sit sae demure on a wee creepy stool,
  And con owre my lesson in auld Madie's schule."

ALEXANDER SMART.

I HAVE mentioned that in a hollow a little way north of the place of my birth was a meadow. It extends from the farm of Boghead, on the east, to some distance westward of Craighall, and one of my very earliest recollections was seeing the whole meadow aglow, one morning in the early summer, with the golden-coloured meadow blooms, and which I thought so exceedingly beautiful that the place, as I then saw it, is vividly before my mind's eye to this day. Another incident which, with better reason, fixed itself in my memory was hammering with one harrow tooth (or tin as they are locally called) upon another and smashing the nail off one of my fingers in my early (and still rather lasting) recklessness. Then followed the fall of my father's thatch barn, not during a storm, but on a calm summer day, when the dust from the dry rotten thatch almost choked those of us who ran out to see. And then, in the autumn after, a sudden and terrific thunderstorm came on when I was lying at the side of a stook of oats, while the harvesters were busy at work among the yellow corn reaping the grain with their sharp polished sickles, the nimble lightning gleaming so appallingly on the bright steel that they cast them away, and as great hailstones at the same instant came rushing through the darkened air and rattled on the face of the affrighted earth, all the reapers ran and sought shelter where they could, and the yellow collie dog, " Help," hastily coming to me in the centre of the stook, where I had crept, put its paws over me greatly to the allaying of my fear in the time of that appalling storm, always, and to this day, remembered as " the chapel shower," from the name of the field in which the harvest operations were then going on.

After having been for thirty-one years in Craighall, under the Duke of Portland (and where all his children were born and registered in the session-books of Mauchline by Andrew Noble, the clerk, who was also clerk in the Rev. Mr Auld's time, and who made the entries when Burns and Jean Armour were before the session),[1] my father at Whitsunday, 1826, removed to the farm of Barrshouse, on the estate of Gilmilnscroft, in the parish of and near the village of Sorn. Being contiguous to the mansion-house, he also afterwards rented the field which had formerly been the home farm. The scenery there is beautiful, looking down, as it does, upon the Sorn village (the most picturesque of any in Ayrshire), and also looking directly over upon the ancient and equally picturesque Sorn Castle, with the river Ayr flowing through the quiet valley with gently swelling heights on either hand. The soil, however, was anything but fertile, being thin and bare, and with a cold sub-soil of stiff, stony clay, which made farming a laborious and anything but a profitable business on such land; but my father then, though in his fifty-eighth year, was still strong and agile, and well-skilled in agriculture as the times then went, and a most willing worker; and Colonel Farquhar Grey, who was then the proprietor, told him, when he took the additional land, to go on, and he would not see him lose by his new venture. The good Colonel's death soon after, however, very much blasted my father's prospects, and hindered his success. His first year in the farm, (1826) was long

---

[1] The late Rev. Dr Edgar, of Mauchline, showed me the entries and commented on the beautiful handwriting, but did not know whose it was till I informed him, knowing it at once from the extract of the births of my father's children in my possession, with Mr Noble's name signed to the extract.

known as "the droughty year" or "the year of the wee corn," for hardly any rain fell from the time the oat crop was sown until it was reaped, and none whatever from the time the barley or bere was sown—then a common crop—until it was cut and in the sheaf, most of the last-named grain ripening in the shot blade or hose, and never coming into the ear at all; while, save on marshy land, the oat crop was so short in the straw that it could not be reaped with the sickle—then the only reaping instrument in use—but had to be pulled up by the roots like the flax crop. The hay crop also was correspondingly light, for not only did no rain fall the whole summer through, but the heavens being continually cloudless, the sun glared fiercely down upon the dry and parched earth during the long summer days from sunrise till sunset; and but for the night dews, which, however, were unprecedentedly heavy and abundant, there would have been no food at all for the flocks and herds in the fields. This was the first year I tried to handle the reaping hook, not that I was then at all fit for such work, which was one that required considerable skill, but one day, unobserved, I got hold of one of the sickles and set to work myself to try and cut the grain and make sheaves like men and women. But I soon made the surrounding woods ring with my wild yells, for I had given myself a great cut on my little finger, which, with the blood running from the wound, made me think it was off altogether. The sickles then mostly in use being what were then called "teething hooks"—that is, the edge was dentated or made with very small and sharp teeth, which made the cut on my little finger all the more severe. My father, who was soon at my side, bound up the wound, and cheered me by telling me that I would one day become a "grand shearer," because it was a saying and a belief that all who cut their little finger when they began to learn, "learned fair," and became most expert reapers; and this I really in after-life became, though I hardly think that the cutting of my little finger—the mark of which is still on that member to this day, nearly eighty years after it was received—had anything to do with my proficiency at the art in after-life.

The almost total failure of the hay and grain crops that season caused a great scarcity of fodder during the following winter, hay and stray not only rising to famine prices, but in many districts they could not be got for money, so that farmers were in despair as to how to get their cattle fed and brought through the winter at all; and many had to resort to cutting the green and succulent whin or furze bushes, and after bruising them with a mallet on a hard floor, or pounding them in a mortar, giving them to the cattle, which they ate with relish and throve upon and were healthy.

It was from Barrshouse that I was first sent to school—the parish school of Sorn, situated at the eastern end of the old bridge which spans the Ayr water, close to the old meal mill still standing. Besides the mill, with its dizzying water wheel, and its soft, dull, monotonous sound, there was also a smithy within an easy stonecast, on the other side of the road from the school, of which crusty old David Boyle was then the blacksmith; and between the mill and the smithy lived douce Peggy Barbour, who sold blackman, peppermints, ballads, bakes, bawbee-scones and bools, etc., and whose little shop those of the children who could command a copper or two were in the habit of frequenting daily. About a hundred yards further to the east was Greenfoot, the cleanliest, tidiest looking country inn I have set eyes upon. It was then kept by palsied, old Hugh Baird, who was also a farmer in a small way. Greenfoot was situated almost under the shadow of Sorn Castle, and quite near to the confluence of the river Ayr and the Cleugh Burn, the former the theme of immortal song, and the latter the traditional scene of horrid murders and crimes, the recital of which made my blood run cold; especially, too, when its rocky linns and black swirling pools were most confidently said to be haunted by uneasy spirits, and consequently it was only at noonday and in company that any of us boys ever ventured to traverse and explore this exceedingly beautiful and romantic defile.

The schoolhouse was, as it were, indented into the churchyard, with windows looking into it from the back and at the end, with the graves of many generations risen much above the floor of the little school of only one apartment. The schoolmaster's house, of two stories, but thatched, stood at the eastern end of the school, with its face, not to the road, but looking into a large and well-kept garden. The schoolmaster then was good old Adam Smith, a little man of stern aspect, very lame, one leg being drawn up and much bent at the knee. He could, however, walk at quite a speedy rate, especially when, unfolding his terrible tawse to their full length, he hurried down the school from his desk to punish some delinquent, which he generally did very severely if not very frequently, for he was a most rigid and stern disciplinarian, and kept the best order in his school of any master I have ever known.

Sitting one bright, sunny day at the end window getting my lesson in the "Nine-penny," and also watching old Saunders M'Gowan, the gravedigger and beadle, making a grave close to it, I got a terrible fright, which bred no small commotion in the school. Old Saunders was as like one of those imaginary eastern demons called ghouls, which are said to prey on human bodies, as it is possible to imagine. He was tall, aged, bent, and lean, with a long, bony, and deeply-wrinkled face, with small, fierce eyes, like a ferret, peering from under a red night-cap which he was in the constant habit of wearing. He also wore tattered knee breeches, the exact colour of the clay, without braces, but buttoned tightly round his loins. The old, faded velveteen vest he wore was much too short, so that there was a space between his breeches and vest, covered only by a dingy shirt. His legs were bare, and the heavy shoes he wore were much too large for his feet, and he was thus withal a person very awful for boys and girls to behold; and both—but especially the latter—always kept at a good distance from him when, as they often did, they entered the churchyard. On the day in question Saunders had the grave dug nearly to its depth, and the window being betwixt us I was in no dread of him. The earth had been cast up higher than the window-sill, and close to it, and just as I had my face against the glass, he cast up a large skull which rolled down from off the dry earth and against the window close to my face. So hideous did it look and so unexpected was the act that with a loud yell I rushed to the door and, terror-stricken, ran home to Barrshouse with the speed of a hare.

Mr Smith had a large family, and a sore and a lasting sorrow overtook him in connection with his eldest son, Robert by name, who was for years cashier in one of the Glasgow banks. Proud of his son, whenever " Mr Robert" came out to Sorn on a holiday visit the school was at once dismissed and the children had a holiday too. In an evil hour he was persuaded to take a considerable sum of the money under his charge and, *just for a day*, he was assured, lend it to a bosom companion, who, of course, failed to repay it, and the defalcation being discovered, poor Robert was apprehended, tried, found guilty, and sentenced to a long period of banishment to Botany Bay, then a penal settlement, from which he never returned, so far as I know.

In these days in all our parish schools the scholars of the Bible or Old Testament class began at Genesis and read right through it to the end; and it was said that after that sad, family calamity and disgrace, whenever these words in the 10th verse of the 22nd chapter of Jeremiah were read in the class—"Weep not for the dead, neither bemoan him; but weep sore for him that goeth away, for he shall return no more nor see his native country"—the old man sat down with his face buried in his hands and sobbed and wept sore. I was not very far advanced when I left the good old man's school; but I still remember the names and the residences of a number of those who were then at his school, both boys and girls; but to-day I could not name one, of them all, who to my knowledge is in the land of the living, though doubtless there are some few yet either in this country or abroad. At school, then, learning mathematics, geometry and the higher branches, was a fine young man, a John Struthers, son of Mr James Struthers of Daldilling; and some fifteen or twenty years after I was much struck at reading in the newspapers one morning, that he was drowned by being washed overboard a steamer on the river Euphrates, during a hurricane. He had learned engineering, and this Sorn lad thus had found a watery grave in the far off river which flows past the ruins of the once great and mighty capital of the ancient Chaldeans!

And the truly grand old man—the dominie himself. What of him? Time's silent but still unwearied foot has travelled on for nearly sixty years since he was gathered unto his Fathers, and since his warm heart became but a clod of the valley, his aged remains having been laid to rest in that most quiet and finely situated churchyard, the graveyard of Sorn, and where perpetually —now high, now low—the river Ayr will continue to murmur dirges near his grave until that dread day when

> "The stricken earth shall mourn her streams
>   And dashing rivers dry,
> And like a dirge the trump of doom
>   Shall wail along the sky!"

Never did I expend half-a-sovereign more willingly than in contributing that sum to assist in setting up a decent memorial stone over his grave, which records that for forty years he was schoolmaster of the parish, and that "an excellent scholar and a good man" sleeps below.

CHAPTER III

HERDING THE KYE, LABOUR AND LEARNING

" A pleasant thing it is to mind
  O' youthfu' thoughts and things,
To pu' the fruit that on the tree
  Of memory ripely hings.
To live again the happiest hours
  Of happy days gone by,
To dream again as I hae dreamed
  When I was herdin' kye."

ROBERT NICOLL.

AT Whitsunday, 1831, my father removed to a cottage at East Montgarswood in the same parish of Sorn, he being engaged as foresman or manager of the farm (a small lairdship), for Henry Richmond, the proprietor, who was a nephew of John Richmond, at one time law clerk to Gavin Hamilton of Mauchline, and the friend of Robert Burns. Mr Richmond was a man of some culture, well learned and well read, as I now remember from the books I used to bring him from a library at Catrine. He had also a taste for poetry, and did a little in the rhyming way himself, and even published, or at least got printed, a poem on a robbery committed on a small farmer belonging to the locality called Findlay, at Rachel Brae, a lonesome rocky place about a mile east of Mauchline, then said and believed to be haunted by evil spirits, and dangerous to travellers by night. Although I have not seen the production for more than seventy years, I still remember the opening stanza of the poem, as somehow then it presented a vivid picture of a winter landscape to my mind's eye—

" 'Twas in the time when Boreas' breath
    Wi' biting breezes blaw,
  And ilka glen and knowe appear
    White wi' December snaw."

The uncle I never saw, but I well remember that his nephew had a poor opinion of him as a man, and frequently and without scruple characterised him as one of the greatest of liars.

Mr Richmond had then working to him on the farm two aged men—Andrew Walker, a brother of Thomas Walker, the poetical tailor of Ochiltree, who addressed the well-known rhyming epistle to Burns; and James Dunlop, the tenant of another small farm of some twelve acres extent, of which Mr Richmond was also proprietor, Little Blackdyke by name, about a mile distant. James had formerly been tenant of the much larger farm of Bruntwood, or Bruntwoodhill, in the neighbourhood of Galston. He was the finest pattern I have ever seen of a Scottish peasant farmer. Though then over seventy years of age he had a fresh, ruddy, cheerful countenance, and though but low in stature, his well-built frame indicated that he had once been possessed of great strength, and this, by report, was equalled by his great courage and daring, for like so many country people then, having in his young days been engaged in the smuggling business, he had once broken the arm of an excise officer who had seized the bridle of his horse when he was riding by in the dark with a cask of brandy or whisky behind him. His tales of the olden time were many and stirring, and related mostly to encounters with the gaugers and their men, and to battles at country fairs, when in those days there were no police to interfere. Of Burns he had a vivid recollection, having, along with a brother, assisted Robert and Gilbert in the formation of a march fence between the farms of Lochlea and Fencedyke, Tarbolton. His wife was a sister of William Rankin, postmaster, Kilmarnock. Andrew Walker had a nephew, John Walker, a lazy "customer weaver" of blankets, druggets, and such like fabrics for the farmers' wives of the district; but John liked much better to have a daily crack with "Laird Richmond" than to ply the loom down in the little hamlet of Bridgend. John, too, aspired to be a poet, and he certainly wrote verses, which the laird criticised, and sometimes, I remember, praised.

The laird and the Walkers were ardent reformers, and the country then was being greatly agitated on the question of the Reform Bill, the passing of which but very scanty measure, as we have long since seen, was to usher in the Millennium, as many said and thought. My father and old James Dunlop, however, remembering well the appalling horrors of the French Revolution near to the close of the 18th century, looked with fear and dread upon the increase of power which the Bill was to give to the people, though not by any means a very democratic measure; and so, when the Bill had passed and the first election under it took place, their sympathies—though still they had no votes—were on the side of the Conservative candidate, Captain Blair of Blair, and when Mr Richmond went to Mauchline and met Mr Oswald of Auchincruive and on the hustings made a speech in support of his candidature, old James Dunlop, who was a master of sarcasm, could not help saying some particularly cutting things of both the Whig candidate, the laird, his master, and of the whole Whig or Liberal party.

From this place I went to an adventure school at Bridgend, kept by a somewhat aged man who had previously been a stone mason; but old James Begg was not a mason of the Hugh Miller stamp, though fully as orthodox a Christian as he, for, on the Saturdays, when the Shorter Catechism was always gone over from beginning to end, the children repeating question about, when, at the end, any of them would start off and repeat the creed, whenever they came to the words " the holy Catholic Church," Mr Begg dashed the book against the wall—he not being able to see in the word " Catholic " aught else than the Roman Catholic Church, or faith, which he dreaded and hated most heartily.

Although Mr Richmond had excellent and well kept hedges on his farm, yet he must also have a herd for his cows, especially as he sometimes had the one half of a field in crop while the other half was being kept in pasture. Strangely, too, though his hedges were the best and most beautiful in the district, he yet had not a gate upon one of the openings into any of the fields, and so he must needs have a herd for his cows in summer, and so I was engaged for such, and got on very well save when clegs (gadflies) in the hot summer time stung the cattle into madness, and made them run wildly about or rush out at all the open gates, of which there were generally four—one at each side of the fields; and so I was sadly put about to keep the frantic animals from running home or running I knew not where. Always greatly alarmed by thunder and lightning, when at any time some loud and unexpected peal would shake the vault of heaven, I would run more swiftly home than ever did the cows when tormented by the clegs, and leave them to stray into the growing corn or go where they would, and then—only some nine years old—I would leap from among the yellow butter-flowers in great terror, believing that somehow, because of their colour, the lightning would strike more readily where they grew than anywhere else!

It will hardly be credited now-a-days that my father— then considerably over sixty years of age—walked from Montgarswood to the church at Kilmarnock—fully eleven miles distant — nearly every Sabbath day, to hear the gospel preached by good old Adam Brown of the Reformed Presbyterian Church there, who it was that sprinkled the waters of baptism upon my face, and after whom—at his own request—I was named. That place of worship, in Mill Lane is now, I understand, called "Martyrs'" Church; for rather strangely, and surely a little inconsistently, when the people there, and in some other places, relinquished the principles of the martyrs and joined the Free Church, they took the name of those whose faithful contending they gave up for a church of laxer principles.

Returning to school again in winter, I was taken away again from it in spring to carry and set in the young tree-plants, for which Mr Richmond himself made the holes, and with which he was beautifying the surroundings of his then newly built steading of houses—now, like myself, alas! beginning to grow old. Especially do I feel this to be the case now, when I see trees there, which by the dozen at a time, I have carried under my arm, now tall and strong and waving their branches high in the air like the very cedars of Lebanon. It was in reference to my having planted all the trees about East Mountgarswood—a circumstance known to Inspecter Aitken, of the Glasgow and South-Western Railway Company at Greenock, that that genuine and popular son of song addressed to me some capital verses on "The poet who planted the trees," of which the following is the concluding stanza :—

> " Here's success to you then, in your work with the pen,
>   May you still write with vigour and power ;
> Like the trees in the wood that ye planted, ye've stood
>   Many years of both sunshine and shower.
> May you yet sing and shine, till you're ninety-and-nine,
>   Before death gives your thrapple the squeeze ;
> And when life's day is past, may the glory at last
>   Get the poet who planted the trees."

To the cottage we had there was attached a large and productive garden, with trees bearing the finest apples and pears that ever made a boy's mouth water. The place, too, was beautiful in its surroundings, and also in the distant view which it commanded to the south. A field of green lea sloped down to a steep brae, always then kept in hay, and which when sown out for such had a quantity of cowslip seed mixed with the grass seeds, and so always in the Spring or early Summer the brae, which lay right facing the sun, was all aglow with the pretty and fragrant flowers ; while at the foot a considerable stream went singing by on its way to join the classic Ayr, a little below the pretty, thriving town of Catrine. Here and there from the hamlet of Montgarswood Bridgend downwards, were little clumps of trees all along the face of the northern brae ; and nowhere did the birds sing so sweetly or build their nests and bring forth and rear their young more securely. A few years ago I visited the pretty spot and explored its every nook, and stood and gazed in pensive silence on every swirling pool still unpolluted by grim coalpit or steaming, thundering factory, and all as well

C

remembered as if I had only left them yesterday instead of more than half-a-century.   There, still

> " The streamlet hurried on and gave
>   Dark murmurs to the wind,
>   That seemed to blame the heart that thus
>   Could leave its tide behind."

Climbing the braes where the cowslips were still blooming and smiling in the sunlight, I paced the field that led up to my father's cottage, but not only was it roofless but its very walls had been mostly swept away, and

> " The cold, cold damp was on the stone,
>   Where bright the fire once glowed,
>   And the mole had dug her path where he
>   Had knelt to worship God ! "

Yes, this was literally the case, and when I saw it, and mused of what had been and what was now, the thoughts which filled my bosom as memory yielded up its stores were inexpressible, and for a time unexpressed; until at length I grew composed enough to stand upon the very spot where, nightly, he had knelt in prayer at family worship, and ere I was rightly aware of what I was doing I was singing aloud, to my father's one tune—Coleshill— these verses of the 77th and 56th Psalms—

> " The days of old to mind I called,
>   And oft did think upon
>   The times and ages that are past
>   Full many years agone.
>
>   My wand'rings all what they have been
>   Thou know'st, their number took ;
>   Into Thy bottle put my tears :
>   Are they not in Thy book ? "

The day by that time was wearing done; the still, pensive gloaming was beginning to cast its mantle of grey over the earth.   The full moon was just rising and showing her big, round rim over the crest of Blacksidend hill, the dew was beginning to fall and the gowans to close up their bonnie bosoms for the night; away down in the glen the burn was singing its own peculiar tune, unmatched by pipe or string, and the mavis and the merle were also singing as gaily as they had done fifty years before, and in sweet forgetfulness of the storms of winter through which they had but recently passed, and all unconscious, perhaps, of the brevity of the summer, and that returning winter would still their songs and pinch their little stomachs; and drawing a long breath and heaving a deep sigh I returned my hat to my head—for I had uncovered it in memory of those whose faces I would see no more and whose voices I would never hear again among the haunts of living men—and I left the solitary spot, and, walking at a brisk pace, recrossed the Ayr by the old bridge at Sorn Mill, and on and away, and I was soon passing down the long prosaic street of Auchinleck, and in a little while after found myself by " my ain fireside " at Breezyhill.

CHAPTER IV

THE WOODS, THE WATERFALLS, THE SCHOOL

"I sigh to think upon the hours of sinless infancy,
  When earth seemed strewed with bright-eyed flowers, and life a
    revelry;
  When sorrow left no sting behind, and laughter chased our tears,
  And we but smiled as Time coiled round our hearts his chain of years."
                      DR JOHN FRANCIS WALLER.

AT Whitsunday, 1834, my father, with his family, removed north to the farm of Castlehill, in the upper part of the parish of Kilmarnock, but situated on the north-western confines of the parish of Loudoun, and little more than two miles from the town of Galston. My father had taken the place in sub-let from the late Mr John Campbell, of Sornbeg, a tall, gentlemanly-looking person with a face red and beaming like the setting sun in summer, and always, when he was out, mounted on one of the best hunting horses in the country, of which he always kept a number, being then master of the Ayrshire foxhounds, and himself a very Nimrod, always steady in the saddle at least, although his deep and oft potations at other times were thought to have much to do with the dark red colour of his countenance. He was, however, a kind gentleman, and my father and he got on well together. He never took offence at "the old Cameronian," as he called him, for the rebukes he fearlessly administered to him for so often seasoning his speech with words and expressions far beyond the "yea" and the "nay" of Scripture; and he laughed loudly when one day he offered to take me into his stables and bring me up as a budding huntsman, and my good old Covenanting father replied that "he would rather bury his weans twa an' twa a week than see ony o' them a' engaged at sic a wicked ploy."

36

Quarrelling with the factor on the estate, Mr Campbell lost the farm, but my father arranged to stay on as subtenant of the new tacksman—the late Mr Matthew Mitchell of Blackshill, in the same parish, a man of a very different stamp, who frequently and intelligently discussed " The Confession of Faith " with my father, the good men, as I can well remember, occasionally waxing warm over the power of the Civil Magistrate, my father being inclined to allow that functionary " not to use the sword in vain," even in spiritual matters, a thing to which Mr Mitchell entirely objected. Long years have sped on and away since then, and both, I doubt not, have joined the Church triumphant above, and, in perfect harmony, are singing the " New Song " to the Lamb who redeemed them.

Though situated in the centre of a fertile and well-wooded district, Castlehill was then, and is no doubt still, a back-lying and lonely dwelling, being nearly a mile distant from any highway, and quite out of sight of any frequented road. Instead, however, of the place being distasteful to my young mind on that account, it was all the more charming. The house—comfortable, but then with a thatch roof—was situated near to a deep and finely wooded ravine, through which flows the Polbaith burn. The ravine, or " bank," as it is generally called, is nearly a mile in length, from the farm of Polbaith, till some distance westward of Castlehill. All the way the banks are steep, and, on the southern side, sometimes rocky ; and then, at least, the whole of the northern side was clothed with noble trees of ash, elm, beech, and other sorts, underneath whose great and out-spreading branches the copsewood grew thick and luxuriantly. A sweeter spot to wander in down by the brink of the burn, or in the opening glades, was nowhere to be found in all the west. The waters of the stream, drawn from the little rills which come wandering down from the moorlands on the east, pure and unpolluted by any public work with its din and clang of labour, pass on until joining the large brook, they go singing along with a face as clear and bright as the moon and stars by night, which glimmer and look coyly down into its many peaceful pools.   In its way to join the Irvine Water, however, some two miles further on, it goes leaping away over a number of picturesque waterfalls, and down through several whirling, foaming rapids; and nowhere are the shy little wrens so numerous as in the mossy brows and hazelly banks which rise on either side of the stream, in which one is almost ready to believe that the fairies still come to bathe and wash their tiny forms in the glassy water pools which whirl and linger here before the water which forms them sweeps onward to the more open valley below; and that in the short but glorious summer nights they deck themselves with the wild roses, which then bud and blossom there, and gleam in every thicket, before they sail away once more upon the silver beams of the moon ere the dawn of the morning breaks.   Nowhere in the early spring time of the year do the snowdrops bloom more luxuriantly, or the yellow primroses hold the silver dews of night longer in their tawny cups, than in the bank just below Castlehill.   In the golden autumn time, too, the red rowans are to be seen hanging in rich clusters here and there all throughout the glen, while the luscious strawberries and the bramble fruit tempt the truant schoolboys from far to gather and taste their palatable sweets.   Although the place is sheltered even in winter, yet when the rains come pouring down in torrents, or when the snow upon the hills melts and dissolves under the soft south winds, then the waterfalls lift up their voices in wrath, and their wild rush and roar are heard far off on the uplands, or away down in the plains below.

What a delight it was to me, then, after being engaged during the day gathering the stones from off the growing ryegrass, or, when the season was a little farther advanced, in coiling the fragrant hay, to wander down into this peaceful, pretty glen, with my younger and now only surviving brother, Thomas—now spending the sunset of his changeful life in a far off land where shines the Southern Cross —and explore its every nook, peer curiously into some little wren's mossy nest, or those of the other songsters of the wood, none of which we would have harmed for money.

Soon after coming to Castlehill, a most inexplicable and striking circumstance happened to me, which the naturally incredulous will perhaps be ready to deny or to ridicule, but it is just as true as that the hand which now traces these lines will one day crumble into dust. My father, one day, was going over to the farm of Burnhouses, about a mile to the north of Castlehill, of which James Howie, his brother-in-law by his first marriage, and the first of the three last of the name of James, and who died in 1847, was then the tenant. Taking me with him, and not going by the road, we crossed over a height by a place called Old Fosterhill, then a ruined farmstead on the farm of Fairfield. I had never been that way before, nor been at nor seen any of the places which met my view when we reached the height and looked down upon Burn-houses, over upon Moscow, and the extensive prospect which lay stretched out before us. There was the farm-steading with the barn on the opposite side of the road and the water-wheel behind! and there were the Moscow lime-kilns emitting their dull, white smoke, with the little hamlet behind; and I stood still with open-mouthed amazement, for every object was perfectly familiar to me! I had in mind or spirit, though not in the flesh, seen them every one before! and it was a considerable time before I could speak or reply to my father, when he asked what I was staring at and why I did not speak. Only on one other occasion did I experience anything of this strange sort. It was a good many years after, when passing up over the western edge of the wild and dreary Galston Moor, and by the very same way, I believe, that Burns went when returning from passing the night in the manse of the good Dr Lawrie at Newmilns. When I came to the farm of Hillhouse, and looked down upon a little loch in the hollow, where (for it was winter), some few curlers were at play, away east to the farm of Burnawn and south-west to that of Cairnhill, upon which eye of mine had never before rested, every place and every object was as familiar to me as if I had passed years among them, and yet I had never, in the flesh, been there before! Does what Coleridge thus say in his " Table Talk " explain such strange occurrences?—" Most of the coincidences (of dreams) may be readily explained by the diseased system of the dreamer and the great and surprising power of association, yet it is impossible to say whether an inner sense does not really exist in the mind, seldom developed, indeed, but which may have a power of presentiment. All the external senses have their correspondents in the mind. The eye can see an object before it is distinctly apprehended; why may there not be a corresponding power in the soul?" Or does this which he farther says in his first " Lay Sermon " better explain or in any way account for the mystery?—" It ought not to surprise us if such dreams should sometimes be confirmed by the event, as though the dreamer had actually possessed a spirit of divination; for who shall decide how far a perfect reminiscence of past experiences, who shall determine to what extent this reproductive imagination, unsophisticated by the will and undisturbed by intrusion from the senses, may or may not be concentrated and sublimed into foresight and presentiment? There would be nothing herein either to foster superstition on the one hand or to justify contemptuous disbelief on the other." The strange thing is that in neither case had I any recollection of ever having dreamed of any such like places, and yet when in the flesh I stood and gazed upon them I felt as convinced that I had somehow seen them all before, even in their minutest details, as that I was then alive.

But if, as the poet says, " Coming events cast their shadows before," and do so at times even in little things, so do they also in greater matters; and the following dream of my excellent, Christian, and strong-minded mother, with its perfect and exact fulfilment, is one of those mysteries which neither Philosophy nor Science can explain or account for, let them argue and discuss, develop and disclose till doomsday if they have a mind.

It was, as I remember well, one morning sometime in the end of the autumn of this year, 1834, that my mother manifested great concern about a younger brother she had who was then factor to Mr Boyd Alexander, of Southbar, an estate a few miles north of Paisley. Mr Alexander was then also either the proprietor or the shooting tenant of Wellwood House and moors in the vicinity of Muirkirk; and on the morning I have mentioned she told my father, in the hearing of us children, how that she had dreamed that her brother John had been out at Wellwood on business, and being taken ill there was conveyed to the house of another brother—James Gibb, merchant in Mauchline—where he died; she also dreaming that she went there to his funeral, and was greatly struck with the rich mountings of his coffin, which she explained; and as she said that she had dreamed this more than once on the same night, and saw everything most plainly, she was greatly moved as she related what she had seen in her dream. How then were we all struck, and my mother overwhelmed with grief, when word arrived of his sudden illness, and very soon afterwards of his death, he having actually been taken ill at Wellwood, and conveyed to Mauchline, and dying at my uncle's, exactly as my mother had seen in her dream! Incredulous people may say that this was only a " coincidence "; but it is one which the wisest of them all can never explain. Others may call it superstition, but that is a word which is easy to speak but not so easy to define; and I remember that the Rev. C. R. Maturin, the exceedingly able but somewhat eccentric curate of Dublin, somewhere says—" The very first sounds that attract the ears of childhood are tales of another life—foolishly are they called tales of superstition; for, however disguised by the vulgarity of the narration, and the distortion of fiction, they tell him of those whom he is hastening from the threshold of life to join, with whom he must soon be, and be for ever."

From Castlehill I went to Paikshole school, taught by John Brown, the self-educated teacher whom I have elsewhere described, a man of excellent heart, great ability, and marvellous memory, but whose wonderful powers of mind and fine classical scholarship were in a manner lost by his being doomed to labour from the days of his full manhood to old age as the teacher only of a country wayside adventure school. John closed the school every night with prayer, and though his prayers were by no means mere formal utterances, habitually and coldly hurried over, yet well do I remember of his occasional petition that "These children might be able to acquire such a measure of learning as would fit them for whatever station in life they might be called to fill, and which would make them useful members of society." And once, when a dreadful and most fatal epidemic of scarlet fever prevailed in the district, and when in three or four days' time some of those who had been well and at school were in their graves, the good man's prayers were so earnest and impressive, and uttered with broken voice and lips quivering with emotion, that all the children—even ill and rebellious Tam Borland—sobbed and wept as John prayed that the Lord would "stay the hand of the destroying angel, and of the pestilence which walked in darkness, and wasted even at noonday, and that there might be no more breaking in of the sore disease among his little ones." Well do I remember, too, how, on stormy nights, when the rain, the hail, or the blinding snowdrift would be darkening the air, rattling on the glass, and shaking the casements of the windows, how he would entreat the Lord to "protect the children from the inclemency of the weather, and stay the bottles of heaven and the wild winds until they reached their homes in safety." Earnest and rapt though John always was in prayer, yet it was his invariable custom—and in the most literal Scriptural way—to "watch" as well as "pray," for he always did so with his eyes but half shut, and looking out on all parts of the school, and woe be to the heedless, irreverent boy who, instead of joining in the prayer, or at least listening with reverend mien, he caught working pranks at that solemn time, for his hands were made warm enough to need no "pawkies" on his way home, however cold the night. But as, after the manner of their heavenly Father, the grand old dominie chastised them for their good, the few of them who now, after the lapse of more than seventy years, are alive, will, like the writer, most heartily forgive their old master—only now but an handful of dust, but, as I said recently, sleeping his last, long, dreamless sleep in an unknown grave in the quiet country churchyard of Loudoun Kirk.   Therefore let us

> " No farther seek his merits to disclose,
>   Nor draw his frailties from their dread abode,
> (There all alike in trembling hope repose)—
>   The bosom of his Father and his God."

CHAPTER V

THE FENWICK HERD AND PLOUGHBOY

"Oh! years hae come an' years hae gane
Sin' first I faced the warld alane,
Sin' first I mused, wi' heart sae fain,
    On the hills o' Caledonia.
But oh! behold the present gloom—
My early friends are in the tomb,
And nourish now the heather bloom
    On the hills o' Caledonia."

ALEXANDER HUME.

HITHERTO I had never been from under my parents' roof at night, for when I was herding Laird Richmond's cows and assisting to plant his trees, I always got home in the evenings. Now, however, the time had come when I must pass from under their dearly-loved roof-tree and go out to service in earnest, my first place being the farm of Townend of Gree, in the uplands of Fenwick, of which James Dunlop was then the tenant, his father and mother (who had surrendered the lease in his favour) still living, however, at the farm, but in apartments of their own. I was to herd the cattle or work as required, and I did both by turns, liking the latter employment best, although in fine weather I was delighted with the noble prospect which stretched out on all sides round, but especially that obtained when herding on the higher fields, away to the south and west. On the east my view was bounded by Lochgoin, so famous in Covenanting story; but on the west, when the day was clear, I could see far away to the coast, with the glittering and gleaming waters of the Firth of Clyde, with the great ships continually coming and going there, and the rocky peaks of Arran, robed by distance in an azure hue, or bathed in floods of rosy, crimson, or saffron light as the great and flaming sun dipped behind the splintered pinnacles of the lofty Goatfell. Such a glorious picture, with that of the great stretch of finely cultivated country which extended down between me and the coast, like the flowers in Wordsworth's case, often gave me " Thoughts that did often lie too deep for tears." Then, when tending the cows, " my converse was with Heaven alone," as the Ettrick Shepherd (of whom, however, I had not then heard, though it was in that very autumn 1835, that he died) had long previously found when tending his flock, as a youth, on " the hills of Ettrick wild and lone." In fine weather I got on nobly, however, by gazing on the ever-beautiful prospect around me and at a distance, by watching the ever-changing aspect of the heavens, and in listening to the " voice of the desert never dumb "—in the wind sighing and wailing over the bent. But on wet days, and when the mist enveloped the moors and hid every distant object from view, I felt the inexpressible loneliness of the scene and the occupation when away out with my cows in the vicinity of a wild spot called " Meg's Neuk." At such times I must have presented a pretty picture to the eye, as fearsome almost to look upon as " The Brownie of Blednoch " himself, as I wandered there in the mist, or crouched by the side of a turf dyke, barefooted, with my grey plaid about my shoulders, or sometimes with a more primitive garment still—a great rough goat-skin tied round my neck, and bound round my slim little body. I certainly looked a very unpoetic being then—tho' even then I had poetic dreamings—and much more likely to frighten than to woo and win the favour of the nymphs of Parnassus.

Almost the only books which I could then command— and which I carried with me to the fields when the days were fine—were the Bible, " Scots Worthies," and " Fisher's Catechism," the latter the most dull and lengthy of all catechisms I have ever seen. I had also some other literature of the Covenanting times, with good John Howie's " Alarm to a Secure Generation," popularly called " The Fenwick Visions." The latter work, descriptive of great, marvellous, and even terrible sights seen on the earth and in the air of that very neighbourhood, nearly threw me into fits by the impending judgments they were believed to presage to "backsliding Scotland." I really, however, liked the whole, even Fisher when dealing with the most knotty points of divinity, while the historical, and more especially the prophetic and poetical books of the Bible, particularly of the Old Testament, threw me into perfect transports of ecstasy and delight.

Mr Dunlop, my master, was a most excellent and intelligent man, especially on religious subjects, and as pious and sincere as he was intelligent, and he had family worship in his house night and morning, and not at all hurried over either as a mere matter of fashion. An excellent singer, too, of sacred music, he not only sang himself, but strove to make all under his roof to sing well, and also "with the heart and with the under-standing." The houses at the farm then were old and most dilapidated, and the poultry which roosted at night on the byre loft could wander on to that above the kitchen, in which there were some holes of considerable size. One night when family worship was just begun and the Psalm was being raised to the tune of Bedford, it was the 113th verse of Psalm cxix., I remember well beginning, "I hate the thoughts of vanity," when down fluttered a hen into our midst, bringing a shower of dust and cobwebs with her. She had somehow lost her balance on the bauks above and fell fluttering and bewildered through the hole. I can see yet the consternation depicted upon the dim and sunburned faces of every one in the circle; while Jean M'Fee, the Highland servant girl, shouted out, "Oh, gracious Lord!" After the hen had been expelled, Mr Dunlop turned to Jean and said, "That was a very good prayer of yours, Jean, but not very reverently put up." The worship proceeded, I coming in for a good-natured rebuke at the close for my ill-suppressed laughter all the time it lasted, which I excused by pointing to the still affrighted and greatly affronted Jean, and by saying— with a little levity, I fear—that "nae doot it wasna a hen at a' but the witch o' Endor's ghost," the account of which in the First Book of Samuel, chapter xxiii., having been the portion of Scripture read in the morning, and about which a discussion had taken place that night, just before worship began.

My master's father, David Dunlop, was a ponderous but a most excellent old man, being too aged, heavy, and frail to go much to church, that of the Rev. Mr Orr of the Secession Church at Fenwick, but his wife, a wiry little woman, being generally driven thither, old David was usually left alone in the house on Sabbath, and it was not without both awe and reverence that I would listen to him singing the grand old songs of Sion—the Psalms—to the solemn old tunes of York, Norwich, Walsall, Coleshill, and others, with his frequent and earnest prayers, when he was unconscious of any one hearing him save the God whom he served, and whose praises and prayers, I have no doubt whatever, ascended right up and away, as sweet incense, into the listening ear of Jehovah.

Once, when in this place, I had a very narrow escape from a large and dangerous bull. I was herding the cows on that part of the meadow which lies, or at least then lay, on the south side of the lade or stream which collects, or then at least collected, the water which drove the Balgray Corn Mill, when a bull belonging to the neighbouring farm of Raithburn leaped the march fence and came in amongst the cattle which I was tending. Old James Craig, the farmer, had not long got the animal, having bought him, as he said just then, "to bring his cows in milk," farmers in general being very much less particular about the bulls they bred from than they are now. Certainly Mr Craig had been so when he bought that animal out of a drove passing along the Glasgow road, for he was the ugliest brute of the kind I had ever seen then, or since. Of a dark brown colour and of large size, he had a strong, deep chest, was light in the rib behind, hollow above the ears, strong-boned, with a head of large size, small eyes, and with one horn pointing upward and the other downward almost over his eye, and with a great thick, hairy tail which swung over his ill-shaped houghs like the limb of a cedar tree! As he had previously cast ugly looks over into the flock under my charge, and bellowing until he made the welkin ring, I, having no dog, had provided myself with a strong cudgel, and so on the day in question I went courageously to turn him out of the field.   The bull, however, came on fully as courageously to meet me, and as he was not deterred either by my shouting or the flourishing of my cudgel, but with a wild bellow and shake of the head began to run towards me, I thought it wise also to run, but in the opposite direction, and the distance between us being but small when I turned tail and fled.   So run I did with the speed almost of the bounding deer, and I had good cause to do so, for the bull came thundering after me, and I was just in time to reach the largest of some saugh trees which grew along the eastern side of the meadow and to dart up it like a cat when he was within two lengths of me.   The tree was not very high nor very strong, but sufficient for the present to place me out of his reach.   But I had heard dreadful tales of infuriated bulls pawing up the earth with their hoofs until they succeeded in overturning the tree in which someone had taken shelter from their fury and then goring him to death.   This bull, however, was up to no such mode of warfare, or was less revengeful, but with a bellow or two and a fierce and strong expression of his breath through his nostrils he kept gazing at me for a little, and then leaping the fence and into the field on the other side I soon saw that my opportunity had come, for he had got into and was floundering through a quagmire; and knowing the ground and that he could not get easily or speedily out, I got down from the tree, ran up to the brute as he was plunging up to the belly, lent him some heavy blows, until with a desperate effort he had got nearly through the soft ground, when I thought it prudent to retreat and to place the bog between the bull and myself.   Old Mr Craig had seen the encounter between the bull and me from the high ground behind his house and was coming to my rescue, when, just as I left laying on the animal, he got sight of the old man with his red plush waistcoat, and with a louder roar than ever made for him, who prudently turned in time, and getting over a stone fence into the stackyard behind the house escaped. The dangerous brute got no more out and was soon after disposed of.

At the Martinmas term I returned to my parents at Castlehill, and was expecting to get spending the winter at school; but ere a week had gone my father had engaged me with good old William Young of Hemphill, to drive the plough, greatly against my mother's mind, who "wished to make a scholar of me." I was, however, to get to school, which I did, during the first three months, after assisting in the barn in the mornings. Mr Young was a most kind-hearted, Christian man, and also had family worship in his house morning and night. His memory, however, was failing much for things of the present, but he was most garrulous and correct on matters of long past times. Singing right through the Psalms, as was then common at family worship, he gave out the 96th Psalm, beginning with "O sing a new song to the Lord," the first night I was there, and he repeated it night and morning, so that when I left, six months after, I don't think he had got much beyond the same call to "sing a new song to the Lord," in the 98th Psalm! His wife was a noble-minded, lady-like old woman, and to me they were both most kind; and forenoon and afternoon Mr Young came from her with cheese and oatmeal cake to me, always much more than I could eat. Though the horses would gladly help me to consume the bread, they would not mouth the cheese, and as I thought it sinful to cast it away, I was always glad when a beggar came my way to whom I could give both.

Next summer again I was back at the Gree with Mr Dunlop. That (1836) was the most cold and sunless summer and the latest and worst harvest I have ever seen. Snow fell before a large part of the oat crop was cut, and consequently much of it was never reaped at all, and when I returned for the second time to Hemphill at Martinmas, a large portion of the oat crop there was still unstacked. The field there on which the most of the crop was then standing was called (and likely is

D

still called) " The Bonnets," as Mr Young informed me, from the showers of bonnets which were confidently said to have been seen falling in the uplands of Fenwick, Eaglesham, Kilmarnock, and some other parishes, and on that field particularly, with many other marvellous appearances, such as armies fighting, or soldiers drawn up in battle array; and of which John Howie thus wrote in the year 1780—" These remarkable appearances, seen in Fenwick parish, were before the Highland invasion in the year 1745. Those relations in the years 1754 and 1755, were just before the beginning of the late war with France and Spain, wherein so much blood was shed; and all the subsequent relations fell out either a little before or during the present war. And show me from history any extraordinary event or revolution that has fallen out in any kingdom, commonwealth, etc., since the destruction of Jerusalem, but what has been ushered in with some remarkable appearance of one kind or another. It is true that they are not mentioned by every historian; but what one author omits is often observed by another."

Old Mr Young was an implicit believer in the supernatural, and related that once, many years before, he had himself both seen a sight and had heard words spoken to himself at Old Hemphill (which stood a little nearer to the hamlet of Moscow than the present steading), and that which was spoken to him he confidently declared was only known to himself and one other then in the spirit world. He would never tell what was the sight he saw, or what it was that was spoken to him there in the grey gloaming.

As a corroboration of what the poet Burns says about turning over " sax roods a day with the plough," I may here mention that Mr Young pointed out to me four great, high-gathered rigs of land containing five roods, and which he said he had ploughed in one March day by a plough drawn by four horses (he and the adjoining farm of Dykescroft then " marrowing "), and had time, the same afternoon, to bury a beggar who had died at the latter farm.

The summer of 1837, I was engaged with a fine old farmer—Matthew Currie and his son Robert—who then succeeded him, at Townhead of Gree, Fenwick. They had a peculiar custom of reading, double verse about, exactly ten Psalms of the metrical version, every Sabbath morning after breakfast and family worship. When we came, however, to Psalm 119, each of the parts into which it is divided was wisely counted as a separate Psalm. When in this family I sometimes attended the parish church with young Mr Currie and his young wife—a daughter of Mr Dunlop's of Floak. A Mr Crosbie was then the minister, and his sermons were of almost interminable length, and, to me at least, and to all others I believe, were as difficult to understand as the cabalistic writings of the Jews. He soon after went to London and joined the Irvinites, and died a few years after: and no wonder, for such long, dull, mysterious sermons would have killed a man with the iron constitution of old Parr himself in the midtime of his days !

During the following winter I served at the farm of Burnhouses, with James Howie, father and son, and was there during the following winter also ; and when there, on the morning of the 7th of January, 1839, I heard and was an actor in by far the greatest storm of wind I have ever seen. It was a Monday morning. We had been up, as usual, at five o'clock—by the kitchen clock, and it was always kept exactly an hour fast, for what reason I cannot yet divine. We had finished the threshing and the winnowing of the corn, which we always did each week day morning. We had watered and fed the horses, and partaken of our own breakfast. All the time the wind was blowing hard. These things were followed by family worship, when just as we were all kneeling at prayer the wind redoubled its fury, the house shook, the slates of the dwelling-house rattled (all the others were covered with thatch). I rose to my feet and looked out, and saw the thatch from the outer houses flying through the close. I gave the two ploughmen a dig each in the ribs and made for the door, they following ; and the old man, cutting his prayer short, with the son soon followed. Thinking to keep the thatch on the house we got hold of a ladder to plant it against the roof of the byre, which was being bared, but in an instant the tempest darkened, the blasts came up upon us from the north-west with redoubled fury and force, and the ladder was wrenched out of our hands in a moment, whirled round and round high up into the air like a feather, and then dashed down again and splintered into a hundred pieces in the close, we narrowly escaping destruction by running into the mouth of a shed. The bonnet was blown off my head following the ladder high up into the air, but, unlike the ladder, it came not down again, so far as any of us could see, and it may be hanging high up on the horns of the moon to this day for aught that was ever again seen or heard of it. The devastation wrought on houses and among woods by the hurricane, which lasted but a short time, was incalculable, and un-paralleled in my time, either before or since.

At Burnhouses then there was a capital collection of books stowed away on a loft, and left to the spiders and their webs, until, as the days grew longer, I dislodged the one and cleared away the others, and almost read my eyes out in the gloaming hours, reading in wonder and delight Hume's and Smollett's "History of England," Milner's "Church History," and other standard works of the kind, to which I had hitherto been a stranger.

In this, as in most other farm-houses at that time, the food of the servants, though in a way abundant, was of the coarsest kind, and when, having got dinner at one o'clock and having to wait till eight at night for supper, which consisted only of beat potatoes and milk, both men and boys were hungry enough; and though in a large meal chest in the loft where I slept there were kept the oatmeal cakes, which then, and even eaten alone, would have been sweet unto the taste, I never purloined any for myself, but once a young Highlandman, a man-servant, urged me to pilfer a cake for him, which at last I consented to do. The chest in which the meal and the bread were kept was a very large one with a great and heavy lid, and at the time, it being nearly empty, I had to bend far down to come at the bread, when down came the heavy lid upon me, taking me such a blow on the small of my back that I thought for a moment I was cut in two, and that the upper half of me would momentarily tumble into the chest and the under half would drop back upon the floor! In a moment or two, however, I began to feel that I was in one piece after all, and not in two halves, and managing to free myself from the weight upon me of the heavy lid, so soon as I got free I fear I implored anything but blessings upon the head of every hungry Highlandman from Arran to lone St Kilda—

" Placed far amid the melancholy main."

And so began and ended my first and last attempt at stealing, if theft indeed it could be called. I had my bed and slept alone in this large and dingy loft, which extended the full length of the dwelling-house, boiler and milk house, and which was reached by a moveable ladder, to descend which in the dark mornings I had to grope my way with great caution, else I might have descended head foremost. The loft was unplastered, and the wind whistled through the unjointed deals without hinderance, and in time of frost, the hoarfrost was visible on the points of every slate nail. My bed would often not be made for a week or ten days; and the blankets, being somewhat full of holes, they in my sleep got round my neck until I was well-nigh strangled. All the cats of the district used to congregate on that great half-empty loft, and serenade me for hours, and many and dismal were the midnight concerts held there by these horrid cats until my flesh was creeping, for from the byre they had easy access to the place where I lay. Such then were the times—" the good old times "—and the care and general treatment given to servant boys then. I perhaps ought to have mentioned, in this chapter, that several of the old men I have referred to in it knew the poet Burns and had occasionally been in his company. This, however, with a reference to the peasantry of that time, as well as to the poet and " The Land of Burns," I shall reserve for the next chapter.

CHAPTER VI

THE LAND OF BURNS: ITS PEASANTRY AND POET

"The hames o' bonnie Scotland,
  While yet the kind were there,
By glen and lea were sweet to see,
  And sweeter still to share.
But the heart o' bonnie Scotland
  Has mony a pang o' pain;
Since what has been in days we've seen
  We ne'er may see again."

HENRY SCOTT RIDDELL.

HAVING in a former part of this work referred to several individuals who knew the poet Burns, and who themselves were afterwards well known to me, when a boy (fine specimens, too, they were of the peasantry of the time of Burns), it cannot but be interesting if I give their recollections of the poet, as heard by me from their own lips, and which in this chapter I shall now do. First, however, I will speak of "The Land of Burns," the exceedingly happy, appropriate, and poetic name given to Ayrshire and Nithsdale by Hew Ainslie, the poet. It is a land which countless multitudes have travelled far to see; for not only have the sons and daughters of Merry England come yearly in thousands to visit the birthplace of Robert Burns, and to gaze upon the hills and the streams that have been immortalised by his muse, but from the Continent of Europe, from distant America, and from the far-off lands which lie beneath the Southern Cross, crowds of people come to worship at the shrine of the rustic genius. Before proceeding to speak of Burns himself, I must look for a little at the diversified features of the land which now bears the poet's name—"The Land of Burns"—and which will continue to do so for evermore. I must speak of the peasantry of these districts, also of the time of Burns, as, beyond a doubt, both had much to do in moulding the

54

character of the man and inspiring him to sing in strains that will never die. Since the time of Burns, the country has no doubt become considerably altered in appearance. The great and the rapid progress made in the science of agriculture has mainly tended to this alteration. Extensive inroads have been made on the large tracts of waste land; and where, formerly, "Nature sowed herself and reaped her crops," the husbandman now casts in his seed and reaps, in autumn, his waving fields of golden grain. But not only has the enterprising agriculturist made great inroads on the wide level wastes of moorland, but in many places, even

> "The mountain's barren brow
> Has now been tortured by the tearing plough."

But the general features of "The Land of Burns" are still the same. Her sternest mountains still stand unscathed by any hand save that of "old Father Time," and even his hand has made hardly any impression upon them. Cassills Downans still wears uninjured its mantle of green. The streams still tumble as tumultuously from the hills and murmur as gently through the valleys as of yore. "Auld Hermit Ayr" still brawls beneath its woody banks and steals round its frowning rocks. The birds still warble sweetly on "the Banks and Braes of Bonnie Doon," and the broad, clear waters of the Nith still go gushing down between its green pastoral hills and its bosky banks. The hawthorns still bloom as gaily and smell as fragrantly in Lugar's classic vale as when the poet sang of their charms and his large lustrous eyes drank in their delights. The blue lakes of the district, which every here and there "steal out suddenly like stars, as moonbeams go to rest," sleep among the hills and reflect their broad shadows on their bosoms, or leap beneath the Winter's storm. The heather bells still bloom on the moorlands and the bluebells still wave by the mossy stream, the wild rose still adorns the thickets and the "crimson tippet" daisy still stars and gems the green lea-rig. Our land, then, is still a "meet nurse for the poetic child"; and though we have poets still who can sing well her charms, yet we have none now who can string so well that noble and deep-toned harp which was unstrung at the death of Burns.

More marked than the change which has taken place in the aspect of the country since the era of Burns is that which has occurred among the people—particularly among the peasantry. He, happily, appeared just in time to catch those manners and customs which were fast dying out and disappearing, and he brought with him for the work transcendent ability, genius, and an ardent desire to perpetuate their manners and customs to all future times.

That Scotland has still a noble peasantry, none who, like myself, have been brought up with and mingled among them will deny. But I question greatly if, in general, her peasantry now are equal to those of the 18th century for warmth of heart, simplicity of manners, undeviating truth, patriotism, and piety. Of course, they were not all such; for there were foul hypocrites of the hateful " Holy Willie " type among them, who were blots upon the fair face of God's earth. And here I may say, in passing, that this person—William Fisher—was well known to both my father and mother, and my father—good Cameronian that he was—used to laugh immoderately at the " Holy Willie's Prayer " of Burns, and would say that, though it was " gey rough," it was as true a picture of the man as any given in the Chronicles of Judah and Israel. Most people know that this canting, tippling creature was drowned in a ditch when going home intoxicated from a Mauchline fair in the year 1809, but few are now likely to know that my own father was one of those who got his body entangled among thorns in a raging torrent about two o'clock on the following morning, his head down and his feet up and only seen, with the water gushing over him, for there had been a great storm of wind and rain during the night. My father's farm was less than a mile from the place, and some of Fisher's family had come seeking him after midnight and had roused my father to go in search of him. It is a curious fact that in the epitaph on Holy Willie, Burns says of him :

" His soul has ta'en some ither way,
    I fear the left-hand road."

and that Fisher actually on his way home that night took the *left hand side* of a fence and ditch near to the farm of Meikle Auchinbrain and so was drowned, for had he taken the *right hand* and the proper side he would have been safe.   My father sent his man with a horse and cart home with the body to the Tongue, "Holy Willie's" farm in the north-east part of the parish of Mauchline, he himself going on before to break the sad tidings to the new-made widow.

My father knew Burns well, being only nine years his junior, though I do not think they had very much in common.   I am old enough to have known when a lad several other peasant farmers who were born even *before* Burns and who knew him well.   Of these I may name Mr David Dunlop of Townend of Gree, Fenwick, who was born about the year 1753; Matthew Currie, Townhead of Gree, Fenwick, who was born about the year 1755; and William Young of Hemphill, Kilmarnock, who was born about two years before Burns.   These all died in the thirties or early in the forties, and all of them considerably over the age of eighty years.   With all of them I served when a boy, either as a herd among the wilds or as a lad on the farms.   They had all known Burns and had occasionally met him, and had been in his company frequently on market days at Kilmarnock, and with my father, who survived till the end of the year 1850, none of them—I have often heard them say—ever heard him utter an oath, saw him angry, or saw him intoxicated.   The late Mr Thomas Aird—a poet of lofty genius and a noble-minded man—who in 1835 was appointed editor of *The Herald and Register*, Dumfries, and who knew and had talked with many men who knew Burns intimately when there, once told me that there could be no doubt but that "the character of poor Robin had been greatly and most unjustly maligned by the people of the town, as an excuse for their neglect of him, and that beyond all doubt many evil things were most unjustly laid to his charge."   But—what will be thought more remarkable still—I, though then only a child, have a distinct recollection of seeing, and of the personal appearance of my maternal grandfather, James

Gibb, of Auchmillan, Mauchline, the tenth of the line. Born in 1745, fourteen years before Burns, he was for half a century salesman at the limeworks of Auchmillan, belonging to the Barskimming family, and I have heard my mother relate that when at Mossgiel Burns would occasionally come with two horses and carts for lime, and how he and my grandfather would have many a good-natured argument on religious subjects, particularly on the Socinian views set forth in an essay published by the Rev. Mr M'Gill of Ayr, on whose side Burns ranked himself, though, as my mother said my grandfather thought, very much for the sake of argument, in which, however, she believed he came off but second best, old James Gibb being full of Boston's "Fourfold State," Matthew Henry's Commentary, and with the far greater "Living Temple" of that greatest of all the Puritan divines, John Howe, and of course with the "Book of Books," the Bible. My mentally great and most excellent mother (who, unlike my father, had a great taste for poetry, could sing like a seraph, and could repeat from memory more old ballads, I verily believe, than are contained in the whole of Sir Walter Scott's "Border Minstrelsy") was born in 1780. She had a distinct recollection of having seen Burns with his two horses and carts at the limeworks, of his wonderful kindliness and gentleness to his horses, and how, though standing at a distance, they would come up to him at his call, when he would gently rub their eyes, of which all horses are exceedingly fond. I should have mentioned another old man, a day labourer, Andrew Walker, brother of Thomas Walker of Pool, Ochiltree, who wrote an epistle to Burns, and who died at Bridgend of Sorn in 1833, at the age of eighty-two, being therefore eight years the senior of Burns. Old Andrew came occasionally to my father's house, and I have heard him relate how that he had seen Burns and James Tennant of Glenconner, a place about two miles from Ochiltree village, going into the inn there. It is remarkable that not one of all the persons I have named ever saw Burns intoxicated, or angry, or heard him utter an oath.

He *may*, however, have been profane when he really *was* angry, and had good cause to be so; just as crusty old Carlyle is said to have cursed like a Castle-Douglas carter at the Craigenputtoch flitting. A grandson of the " rough, rude, ready-witted Rankine " of Burns [1]—John Rankine of Adamhill, Tarbolton—Hugh Merry by name, and as great a wit, too, as his grandfather, who once came on a visit to me when I was living at Wellhill Tileworks, New Cumnock, and which visit he prolonged to the long period of seven years, told me that he had heard his grandfather say that Burns was the kindest-hearted and the best-natured man he ever knew. It was his daughter, Annie Rankine, the mother of my *dreich* visitor, who was the heroine of that capital song of Burns, beginning, " It was upon a Lammas night." She died at Cumnock so recently as 1843, at the age of eighty-four years, so that she was born in the same year as Burns. At the request of a sculptor in the town I recently wrote an epitaph which he was desirous of carving upon her tomb-stone, but a descendant of hers—one, perhaps, of the " unco guid "—would not allow it, though urged to let it be done by some of the best and most religious men in the town. These are the lines :—

> " Ah ! Annie, now, how changed thy lot,
> Since 'mong the corn rigs bonnie,
> Ye romp'd and ran, a lassie gay,
> As blithe and loved as ony.
> To thee, like Burns, Death came, and call'd,
> Nor would he treat or parley;
> And here ye spend a long, dark night,
> Where bloom nae rigs o' barley."

That Burns was " slow to wrath " and also guarded in his speech, according to all the excellent authorities I have named, would seem, however, to contradict, at least in part, the charge which Thomas Walker, already referred to, makes in his " Epistle from a Tailor " to Burns, in which epistle he was almost, however, to a certainty assisted by William Simson—the " Winsome Willie " of

---

[1] Appendix No. 1.

Burns—then schoolmaster at Ochiltree, although the whole poem rises little above doggerel. Well do I remember the appearance of those ancient men of the Burns period — their strong mother - wit, their large measure of commonsense and their pithy sayings; their antique dress, knee-breeches; their broad-tailed blue coats, with bright metal buttons; their broad blue bonnets, with tops on them like red double poppies in bloom; and with clear, often silver, buckles on their shoes. They were also for the most part honest, truth-loving, and upright men; and in every house in the country then, and in most of those in the towns also, was to be heard, morning and evening, the voice of Psalms and prayer. Burns, whatever his views might be of creeds and confessions, kept up the grand old custom in his household too; while the broader and grander sympathies which he possessed above most others are seen in such lines of his as these—

" But deep this truth impressed my mind,
  Through all His works abroad,
The heart benevolent and kind
The most resembles God."

Burns entered the field of Scottish song at a time when that field was almost unoccupied. No writer of much eminence had appeared in it since the death of Ferguson, which took place twelve years before Burns appeared as a poet. Indeed, from the time of Allan Ramsay, Scotland had produced no poet who excelled in the native dialect save Ferguson. A few gems had indeed been thrown off during that period, such as the beautiful ballad of " Auld Robin Gray," the two versions—alike charming and pathetic —of " The Flowers of the Forest," and the fine racy song of " Tullochgorum," and a few others by the Rev. John Skinner. During this period Scotland indeed produced not a few poets of exalted genius, whose works were, and are still read and admired, but most of these were written in English, and among the best of these poets we may name the philosophic Beattie—whose " Minstrel " was read and admired by Burns; and the gentle, melancholy, consumptive

Michael Bruce, author of the " Ode to the Cuckoo," and other pleasing poems, and who, since his death, has fared so ill at the hands of false friends and some modern critics. There can be no doubt but that the early poems of Burns were written after the manner of Ferguson, for whose writings he expressed great admiration. But his genius was too original, too lofty, fertile, and aspiring to submit long to the mere art of imitation. He soon, therefore, struck out a path for himself by which he was to reach immortality, and leave far behind not only the bard at whose feet he had at first deigned to sit, but every previous poet of his native land. There is nothing, I think, more plain or more pleasing in the life of the poet, than the very apparent fact that Burns was, at first, wholly unconscious of the genius and the powers he possessed ; and indeed amid all the loud bursts of popular applause which greeted his ears when the lion of the *literati* of Edinburgh, or at any time in after life, he seems never to have been fully aware of his own genius and lofty powers. He could not but know that he had indeed written some things " that the world would never let die," but that he ever dreamed that his name was to be pronounced with love and admiration during all the coming ages, and wherever the English language is spoken, I do not believe. Nor did he foresee that his productions were to exercise a mighty influence on the literature of the English-speaking world, long after the hand which had penned them had crumbled into dust, and when in that great and fertile brain of his which had given them birth, " the worm alone would be living where rapture had been ! "

It is not my province here to deal with the beauties of individual poems, though I cannot refrain from doing so in regard to one or two of them, though in a very cursory manner. " The Vision," then, I look upon as one of his very best poems. The opening stanzas are somewhat sad in tone, but picturesque and beautiful in language. The eye of day had closed far in the west, and the daylight had ceased to linger on the western cloud ; the curlers had left off their roaring play, and he, tired with wielding all day long " the thresher's weary flinging tree "—the flail—a most toilsome kind of labour, and with which the grain in those days was separated from the straw, and of which I myself knew something in my boyhood. Seated in the " spence " and musing in pensive mood, his thoughts reverting to the past, and thinking what might have been, he was about to take an oath to give up for ever the unprofitable business of verse-making when, as he relates, Coila, the Scottish muse, stood before him, and prevented the rash vow. Pourtrayed upon her mantle were many of the scenes of his native land, that land which had first inspired him to sing and taught his lips to hymn those songs of love, friendship, and patriotism, which shall ring round the world to all time, chanted by the ten thousands of tongues of many lands. There pourtrayed on Coila's mantle were seen the grandest pictures of the land he loved—the rivers, the mountains, the stately towers and palaces, the wild, romantic glen, the hoary ruin, and the borough town (Ayr), which he has immortalised in immortal strains. Throughout the poem there runs a lofty moral tone, more lavish descriptions of the beauties of Nature than is the poet's wont, and a warm feeling of devotion for all that is noble and good. Burns was perhaps less a descriptive poet than we might have expected from his evident love of Nature, and yet he by no means failed in this either ; and, indeed, even in describing scenery, his pourtrayal of it is often almost inimitable, as, for example, this stanza in his charming poem on Hallowe'en :—

> " Whyles owre a lynn the burnie plays,
>   As through the glen it wimpl't ;
> Whyles round a rocky scaur it strays ;
>   Whyles in a wiel it dimpl't ;
> Whyles glitter'd to the nightly rays
>   Wi' bickering dancing dazzle ;
> Whyles cookit underneath the braes
>   Below the spreading hazel."

Reading or listening to such a correct, vivid, and beautiful description as this, who will not say that Burns might and should have been a painter as well as a poet ?

If the pen-pictures he gives us of natural scenery are not very frequent, they are always excellent when he does give them. Of the purely English poems of Burns there is not a more beautiful one than that " To the shade of Thomson, on crowning his bust at Ednam with bays." The verses are of classic yet plaintive beauty. The poet of " The Seasons " was no less a favourite with Burns than he has ever been with every devout lover and worshipper of Nature, and he must ever remain so while the seasons, of which Thomson sang so well, revolve on the wheels of Time. But the poem possesses an interest for us now which the poet could never foresee. When Burns sang of the cooling shades of Dryburgh, little did he think how hallowed that spot would afterwards become in the eyes of the world by being the last resting-place of Sir Walter Scott, a great poet, and, by a long distance, the greatest novelist the world has ever seen. And when he sang of the hills and the stream of " Classic Yarrow," how little did he then dream that an inspired Shepherd of Ettrick was afterwards to tune his reed and give his soul to song, and all but rival his own deep-toned skill; for James Hogg can never be forgotten while " The Bird of the Wilderness " — the Sky Lark — ascends to hail the dawn of the summer morn; and his " Kilmeny " shall be borne along on the current of time, and the angelic melody of its smooth-flowing verse shall ring among the hills and vales of his native land for evermore. It is, I believe, not very generally known that Samuel Rogers, author of " The Pleasures of Memory," " Human Life," and other long popular poems, and Burns came before the world as poets in the same year, 1786, and yet Rogers survived Burns by no less a period than fifty-nine years, dying under the burden of ninety-three years, in 1855; while, thus half a century before, the light and the lustre of the eye of Coila's bard had been extinguished in the valley and shadow of death, and his tuneful tongue silenced by death's pale seal being set upon his lips.

I must not wait to take any particular notice of any of the other poems of glorious Robert Burns. Let me say, however, that in that great poem, " Tam o' Shanter," are many couplets of remarkable power. Who that has ever been abroad during the darkness of night in the thick gloom of a thunderstorm but can feel and understand the appalling picture presented to the mind's eye by those two lines :—

> " The speedy gleams the darkness swallow'd,
> Loud, deep, and lang the thunder bellowed."

Was there ever a more tender and touching "lament" than that which Burns breathed upon the wandering winds for James, Earl of Glencairn? His " Lament of Mary Queen of Scots " is not less touching. The effect of this pathetic poem is greatly heightened by the beauteous drapery in which all Nature is therein clad—the far-spreading greenwood, the glistening streamlet, the azure skies, the little daisies which "star like snowy gems the lea," the lark carolling at the gates of morn, the merle piping in his woodtide bower or in the blooming haw-thorn by the cowslip-covered bank, singing drowsy day to rest, are the beauties with which it is embellished, and as if thinking of these the poet makes the imprisoned Queen exclaim—

> " The meanest kind in fair Scotland
> May rove their sweets amang ;
> But I, the Queen of a' Scotland,
> Maun lie in prison strang."

Of the cruel conduct of the great but jealous and vindictive Queen Elizabeth to the beautiful Queen of Scots I cannot trust myself to say a word. Of his powerful and scathing satirical poems I may not here speak. Most, if not all, of them were productive of much good. Nor would I do more here than simply refer to the songs of Burns, the best the world has ever seen, or perhaps, and too likely, will ever see again. These songs are admirably suited to men in every position or circumstance of life. The home-sick exile, with a tremulous voice and a tear in his eye, sings of " Craigieburn " and the " Banks and Braes of Bonnie Doon "; the lover sings of his charmer ; and the soldier on a distant shore, of the time " When wild war's deadly blast is blawn"; and the poor, and often despised, but honest man sings how " A man's a man for a' that"; and never while the wild flowers wave on the hills of Caledonia, or her blue lakes tremble in the summer breeze or leap beneath the spirit of the storm which shrieks from her snow-clad mountains, shall the songs which he has bequeathed to us and to all time, be forgotten or cease to thrill the human heart. Generation after generation shall pass away from the stage of time into the land of deep forgetfulness, but in every generation there shall be multitudes to love the departed poet, and be delighted, cheered and benefited by his productions.

Ere I close this chapter I cannot help referring to the cold neglect, and even the " cutting scorn," which to such an extent wounded the spirit of Burns when alive, and comparing these with the honours now being everywhere heaped upon his memory when, now, alike to him is the voice of praise or blame. Someone in speaking of the proverbial poverty of poets, and their too generally unhappy lives, thus truly says :—" Every age has heard, with pleasure, its *predecessor* arraigned and condemned for cruelly neglecting some hopeful man of genius, whom a little attention would have rendered comfortable and happy, and who, in return, might have instructed and delighted his country by the exertion of his talents. But while the sentence is passing, some unhappy son of song and man of noble and original genius is just being treated in the very same way; and may already be approaching that miserable catastrophe that shall lay as just and as perfect a foundation for a similar charge and a similar sentence in the ages to come." Yes, and notwithstanding all the mighty fuss which now is being made about doing honour to the memory of Burns and the incalculable sums which are being expended in erecting statues of him and monuments to his memory, it is just the old story of how

" Seven cities now contend for Homer dead,
    Through which the living Homer begg'd his bread."

E

For were it possible for Burns to return again to earth, but his identity to be unknown to anyone, and though he should manifest a double measure of genius and power to that which he now manifests in his works, they would be as slow as ever to recognise his merit and his talents; look coldly upon him, and might not even give him the meanest place in the Excise—that of a gauger! This is made perfectly clear by the proceedings which we continually see at these Burns monumental movements of the present day; for while those who take the lead in them and sing and shout about " honest poverty " and about how

> " An honest man though e'er sae poor
> Is king o' men for a' that,"

it is not any such whom we ever find being asked to the front at such " inaugurations," however well he may have sung, or no matter what rolling thunders of eloquence he may be known to be possessed of. It must be then (as it always is) a rich man, or a titled magnate, who must be called on to show forth and to proclaim the worth of the poet of the " Lords of Labour! " The matter, as regards Burns and numbers before his day and since, has thus been aptly put by William Reid, a modern poet :—

> " The starving poet, when he asked for bread,
> Was rudely told to wait till he be dead ;
> And when the grave had decomposed his bones,
> His soul would have a feast of chisell'd stones."

Yes, all this praise and flattery of Burns nearly, save the brief and fitful blink which shone upon him in Edinburgh at his first visit there, when he was gazed upon as a sort of nine days' wonder, and then neglected, if not despised, and at last left to die a poor, ill-paid gauger, was and is but noise and show. Yet the poet is praised and lauded to the skies now, when his clay-wrapped heart, down yonder at Dumfries, is no longer conscious of the honour. Had but a one-thousandth part of what has been expended in raising statues to his memory within the last few years been bestowed upon him when in life, how it would have cheered his weary heart and kindled afresh the fading brightness of those large, lustrous eyes of his, which were so soon to be extinguished in the valley and shadow of death. His most true and fervent admirers, however, though they may not be able to do much to "build his sepulchre or set up his statues," can still from the depths of their hearts say, with another poverty-stricken poet, now deceased—

" O ! blessed be the brawny arm that tore presumption down,
  That snatch'd the robe from worthless pride and gave to toil a
    crown ;
  That smote the rock of poverty, with song's enchanting rod,
  Till joy into a million hearts in streams of beauty flow'd.

" There may be grander bards than he, there may be loftier songs,
  But none have touch'd with nobler nerve the poor man's rights
    and wrongs ;
  Then, while upon the hazy past the eye of fancy turns,
  Raise high the fame and bless the name of glorious Robert
    Burns."

CHAPTER VII

LABOUR, LITERATURE, AND LOVE

" 'Tis ever pleasant to rehearse
The scenes of youth in prose or verse,
To live again our young life over,
To be once more the youthful lover—
A pensive pleasure mixed with pain,
For ah! we ne'er grow young again."
JOHN FRANCIS WALLER.

AFTER the long digression on Robert Burns in which I have indulged, on those who knew him, and on the peasantry of that time, I now return and continue the story of " my wanderings in this world of care." My parents having removed to the farm of Low Molemount, in the vicinity of Galston, I spent the winter of 1837-38 at school, and during the course of it occurred the longest frost and one of the greatest severity which has ever taken place in my time. In the spring of the year I was engaged to work at the tileworks which then stood close to the town of Galston. My duties were to be what is called a " washer-off" to a tile-moulder named David Ramage, a tall fine-looking man, who resided with his parents at the lodge of Cessnock Castle. He was, in a way, a good master, and a man of considerable intelligence. My wage was six shillings and sixpence a week, and that paltry sum was dearly earned, for on the mornings of every Monday and Tuesday I had to be forward at the works, for the emptying and filling of the tile kiln, at four o'clock or, if but five minutes late, I was fined in the sum of one penny. For the emptying and the filling of the kiln my master received two days' pay for himself and myself, though by working hard it was always accomplished in a day and a half; and while he not only pocketed the two days' pay for me, I had to carry off tiles for the rest of the day without getting any additional pay. Every morning during the rest of the week I had to be at the work by five o'clock, and with barely half an hour for breakfast and no more for dinner, was kept hard at work till seven o'clock at night. The tile-moulders then being paid by the thousand, they thus made slaves of themselves, and greater slaves of their boys, to increase their earnings, which were large, from 7s. 6d. to 10s. a day. Little do the youths of the present time realise how much they owe to the Factory Acts and to the legislation of these later and more humane years, for at the time I speak of masters could treat their workpeople exactly as they pleased.

The view from Low Molemount was exceedingly beautiful. Situated about a mile and a half south-west of the town of Galston, and at a considerable elevation, it overlooked a long stretch of the fair and fertile valley of the Irvine Water, and looked directly over upon " Loudoun's Bonnie Woods and Braes " and the palatial castle which stands in their midst. Half a mile to the west was the old historic castle of Cessnock, from the tower of which we could hear the clock striking the hours while sitting at our own fireside. To the east was Loudoun Hill, heaving its ridgy back above the plains below like some huge elephant guarding the entrance to the wilds, which stretch away eastwards towards the town of Strathaven, and which overlooks the battlefield of Drumclog, where the brave and lion-hearted Covenanting peasantry routed the ferocious Graham of Claverhouse and his equally ferocious troopers, and of which the amiable and talented Lady Flora Hastings thus wrote :—

" Smile not, O sons of these pacific times !
When, free to worship even as ye list,
Ye think upon the motely mustering
Of those who, for the Holy Covenant,
Raised to the Lord of Armies one loud Psalm,
And on the purple heather of Drumclog
Pour'd forth their blood to seal their faith thereby."

From the higher ground, a little way south of our dwelling, we could see the waters of the Firth of Clyde shining and glowing like burnished gold in the setting sunlight, as the western beams of the great crimson orb seemed travelling towards us from afar "in rings of welling light." Directly south, on the farm of Middlethird, the curious and inquiring wanderer could trace the remains of ancient Druidical mounds, while down below the waters of the little brook of Burnann, so celebrated for its pretty pebbles and jaspers, brawled beneath its bosky banks of hazel, hawthorn, and birch, where the birds sang the earliest, the sweetest, and the latest, and the cuckoo's pleasant but plaintive cry was heard all throughout the nights of the opening summer. Sometimes, though seldom, I got released from toil on the afternoons of Saturday, when it was my delight to wander waist-deep among the yellow broom till

> "The stars would shine o'er day's decline,
> And tell the hour of love."

Part of the following winter I again spent at school, and next summer I went to labour at the Lanfine tileworks, which then stood a little way south of the town of Newmilns, on the farm of Mount Pleasant. The proprietor of Lanfine—Mr Brown, father of the recently deceased and excellent lady, Miss Brown—was nearly related to the celebrated Lord Jeffrey. Once when visiting at Lanfine, and when driving past with Mr Brown, they stopped and walked through the tileworks together, and when passing and halting for a little while where I, barefooted, was carrying off the new-made tiles, Lord Jeffrey looked at me and smiling said, "That takes nimble work, my lad," to which I only answered by a smile. That was the only time I ever saw the brilliant but caustic Edinburgh reviewer, the eloquent advocate, and afterwards the upright judge. His nephew, Mr Thomas Brown, younger of Lanfine, used to frighten me then in my occasional rambles through the extensive plantations which grew far along the hillsides to the south of the tilework; for he nearly always carried a great open clasp knife in his hand, not of course for any homicidal purpose, but to lop off an unsightly or offending twig, I believe, when it met his eye in his frequent and lonely walks through the woods; although some of the wild weaver lads of Newmilns would tell how he had threatened them and chased them with his great open "cully" when he came upon them in the plantations. Notorious poachers many of them were, and no doubt he knew it and likely enough desired to frighten them from entering the woods. It was only in the open glades in the woods that I ever wandered and once when he met me there he said—though not at all sternly—"You don't rob birds' nests, my lad, I hope?" To which I replied that I never did and never would, and with a "That's right" he passed on, and so did I. Only once or twice did I meet him again, and again in the woods, and lifting my cap to him he nodded, smiled, and passed on without speaking.

Mr Brown was a man of culture, and was on intimate terms with Thackeray, and had had penetration enough to predict that great man's future success as an author before he became famous. Mr Brown was also a poet, and one of severely classical tastes, and although he never published any volume during his lifetime, a small one containing his poems appeared after his death, which took place in 1873. His muse appeared to delight most in legendary, tradition-ary, or historical scenes and events, and so he has sung thrillingly and well of "The Last Hours of Tiberius," "Margarita Pelagia," "The Legend of St Rosalie," and "Catherine De Medici"; while with great power and exquisite finish he portrayed in a tragedy the dark career of Borgia, that symbol of blackest vice and deepest infamy. His taste and culture may be seen in the following brief song in "Margarita Pelagia":—

"The choral hymn, the cloister dim
    For those who choose to sigh;
For me, for me, the vine-hung tree
    Shall be my canopy.

"Come, Hebe fair, with braided hair
    And rosy cup of joy;
Come, Cupid, play thy roundelay,
    My merry minstrel boy!

" 'Tis Nonus thine to mope and pine,
    O'er tear-soil'd beads to moan,
Thy mitre's weight, thy staff of State,
    To all are loathsome grown."

I have given this sample of the poetry of a strange, almost
weird, and original character, because very few have had
access to his works, or are ever likely to have it in their
power to peruse any of them.

The following winter I again spent at school, this time
at the Barr School, Galston, of which Mr H. W. Kilgour,
a man of no great learning but of cultivated tastes, gentle
disposition, and the most kind and excellent Christian
principles, was then the master, with whom I made rapid
progress both in learning and in love for, and an acquaint-
with, polite literature.

During the three following summers—those of 1840,
'41, and '42—I was engaged at the tilework of Windyhill, also near to the town of Newmilns, and latterly as a
moulder, making good wages. Mr Boyd, the master, was
also a farmer, and a good and upright man; and as some
of the family were much about my own age, light-
hearted, friendly, clever, and intelligent, I was much
about the house, and in the family circle by night as well
as by day. The elest son (who died with appalling
suddenness at New York a few years ago, whither he
had gone on a visit to a son) was particularly so. We
read the same books together, and attended in company a
course of lectures on geology by the Rev. (afterwards Dr)
Norman Macleod in the church at Newmilns, then newly
ordained as minister of the parish of Loudoun. These
lectures—as I can now understand—though made most
interesting, were somewhat superficial, but they had the
effect—perhaps intended—of drawing the minds of his
people very much away from " the ten years' conflict,"
then raging, which preceded the Disruption of 1843.
Speaking of this great and good man, I cannot help
referring to a remark made by him in a letter which he
wrote to a friend only ten days after his ordination, in
which he laments that " save among the Cameronians,"
there was " not a vestige of family worship in the parish."

In saying so the reverend gentleman spoke without due knowledge of the country people especially; for in nearly every house then family worship was observed on week days as well as on Sabbath, as I know very well. But in the town it was far otherwise; for while the aged were, for the most part, ignorant and altogether in-different about spiritual matters, the young and the middle aged were nearly all Chartists, free thinkers, and poachers, and many of them blatant blaspheming atheists, defying Heaven and plotting against the Government. There were a few noble exceptions, however, and among these was a certain tailor Paterson, who lived in Greenholm, which, though in Galston parish, was and is really a part of the town of Newmilns. He, however, was a Cameronian, and an elder of that church in Darvel. But there was also Mr Macleod's own beadle and gravedigger, Macpherson by name, who, when I saw him some fifty odd years ago, was then some years over the far fourscore, and, wonderful though it may seem, he had been so long gravedigger that he had buried more than twice the population of the whole parish of Loudoun! He was a good, pious, and intelligent man, and, like tailor Paterson, was greatly gifted in prayer, and both really in this respect far surpassed the young minister, notwithstanding that afterwards, in "The Home Preacher," he published a manual of family prayers. Somehow, and it is strange, men of the greatest ability often fail in prayer, and the wings of the eagles seem clipped when they attempt to soar up into the unseen empyrean of the seventh heaven where the Mercy-seat is.

Once the young and popular but hasty-tempered minister came upon me as I was coming from the Loudoun tileworks, which I had been visiting. I was passing along a footpath through his glebe, which he was trying to stop. I was reading while walking—a custom I still have—and ere I knew he was upon me, and somewhat sternly asked me if I was not aware that there was no road that way. I replied that I thought there was. Looking at me, he asked what it was I was reading. I said it was the "Tales of the Borders," and the one I was reading was "The Dominie's Class." "And do you think them good?" "Charming," I replied; and having asked where I came from and being told, he said, "Oh, Matthew Todd's son. He's a good Cameronian; you may pass." The old church was then standing, and at the summer communions there were always preachings in the churchyard behind the church. These on two or three occasions I attended, and wild and Godless as too many of the Newmilns folk then were, I never saw anything but the best behaviour at these largely-attended "holy fairs," as Burns would have called them. On one occasion the late Rev. Dr Stirling, of Galston, was preaching from the tent in the churchyard, while the communion was being partaken of in the church, and he (though considered a much better scientific engineer than a preacher) riveted my attention, and that of many others also, more than ever the great Norman did. Just about that time the steamboat *President*, the first, I think, that ever crossed the Atlantic, was lost on its return voyage, for it never was heard of. It had a number of passengers, and among them an earl's son, on board, all of whom went down with it. Dr Stirling, taking for his text these words in Isaiah xlv. 22—"Look unto Me and be saved"—began by saying (I remember his very words, look, and voice well): "Had any of you, my brethren, been on board that unfortunate ship, the *President*, which, doubtless, has now sunk beneath the waves of the Atlantic, and when she was rolling helplessly in the trough of the wild waves, and was just about to be engulfed by them— had a voice come to you from across the sea saying, ' Look unto Me and be ye saved'—how eagerly would every eye have been turned in the direction of the speaker?" And he went on eloquently to draw the easily understood inference, and riveted the attention of every one till the close.

Once, and only once, I heard the "great MacKinlay" of Burns preach. It was in Dr Stirling's church at Galston on the evening of the Summer Sacramental Sabbath the year before he died. Even then he had a graceful elocution and a fine musical voice, and to these, mainly, I rather think, was due his great popularity at any time of his life.

At this time I was devouring the wonderful novels of Sir Walter Scott, and luxuriating in his chivalrous and fine descriptive poetry; and many other works of the same kind I then read, though I gave not myself entirely up to such, for I was equally delighted with Stephen's "Travels in Egypt, Arabia, and the Holy Land"—still, save Porter's "Giant Cities of Bashan," the best work on these old historic lands I have ever read. "The Edinburgh Cabinet Library" of history, travel, and biography delighted me, with of course the poems, and also the nearly as wonderful letters of Burns; and, in scarcely a less measure, "The Queen's Wake" and "Pilgrims of the Sun" of the marvellous Ettrick Shepherd.

In these years, while at Windyhill, labour at the tile-work was given up in autumn for that of the harvest field, which, though severe, I liked exceedingly, and became an adept at the sickle. At night, too, after the toil of the day was over, there was no end of fun and frolic among the lads and lassies; indeed, Windyhill was proverbial for its merry "rockings," though these, mostly, took place in the winter months. One of these harvests I spent with Mr Boyd's father-in-law, old James Picken of Parkhead, on the confines of Hareshaw Moor, in the parish of Fenwick, where the merry-makings were quite as frequent, the lads as agreeable, and the lasses as blooming and as bonnie as those of Windyhill. It would have been strange then if a youth of such sanguine temperament and warm poetic feeling and tastes, as formed such a large part of my nature, had not experienced something of the force and truth of what the rather grim and sombre but powerful poet of "The Grave"—Robert Blair—describes as—

"Beauty! thou pretty plaything! dear deceit!
    That steals so softly o'er the stripling's heart,
    And gives it a new pulse unfelt before!"

This I did to the full, though I need not say whether I was "smitten" most among the moors of Fenwick, or by

the bright, liquid eyes, and peachy cheeks of the maidens
of the Irvine Valley. Long years after, in my poem on
" August " of the "Circling Year," I have thus recalled to
memory, and embalmed those happy, happy days in the
following lines :—

" O joyous August ! treasure of the year !
  I love thee, though thou tell'st of winter near,
  Once more, I feel myself a youth again,
  Heaping with golden sheaves the groaning wain ;
  A bright girl cooing near me like a dove,
  My heart first fluttering at the touch of love.
  That sweet-toned voice e'en now I seem to hear
  Still sounding sweeter, as Life's close draws near !
  Her cherry lips, bright cheek, and dimpled chin,
  Her small, round mouth, with faultless teeth within ;
  The raven traces round that polished brow ;
  Those deep-blue eyes (they beam upon me now) ;
  That heaving breast, tempting as Eden's fruit :
  The well-formed waist ; the small and pretty foot—
  All brought a swimming sense upon my brain,
  And made my blood career through every vein.
  A boy no more ; love-lifted, I began
  A new life then—in love a full-grown man ! "

Neither that charmer however, nor one or two others,
perhaps in a scarcely less degree, were destined to become
mine.   There was falseness on neither side, and yet the
Fates (strange Fates !) put and kept us asunder.
    William Motherwell in that most charming of ballads,
" Jeanie Morrison," says of that fair girl :—

" We parted when we baith were young,
      When hearts can ill bear pain ;
   But weel I mind ye sabbin' said,
      We sune sal meet again.
   We sune sal meet !   Where, Jeanie, where ?
      Or when sal that tak' place ?
   'Tis ten lang years since then, and yet
      I've never seen your face ! "

But what would he have said of long separation of more
than sixty years ? Yet such it has been with me, and one

still in the land of the living! Now, however, we can both think kindly of each other, without dreading—like the heroine of the fine, touching ballad of " Auld Robin Gray "—that " that wad be a sin." Others of that once bright, beautiful, buoyant group of then lovely girls are still alive, though their sun, like mine, must now be nearing its setting; and my best and most earnest wish for them all now, " when life has dwindled to its farthest span," is that so beautifully and so piously expressed by that noblest of hymnologists, the Rev. Henry Francis Lyte, and with him may they all be able to say—

> " Swift to its close ebbs out life's little day ;
> Earth's joys grow dim, its glories pass away ;
> Change and decay in all around I see ;
> O Thou who changest not, abide with me."

One of the then happy and unbroken band who took and pressed my hand with tear-filled eyes as I parted with her and bade her farewell when leaving her fine old grand-father's house afterwards got " mated toa clown," with whom she was not happy, has long since paid " the debt of nature," doing so when but young in years, and now she rests in the long dreamless sleep of death, away where the ceaseless waves of Wigtown Bay keep on for evermore "murmuring dirges round her grave." How true is it then, as Tom Moore has so truly and so beautifully said, that

> " All that's bright must fade,
> The brightest still the fleetest ;
> All that's sweet was made
> But to be lost when sweetest."

It is an unspeakable pleasure for me now, at this far distant day, to be able to think and to know that all of these then fair, lovely, and loved ones, like the " Bonnie Kilmeny " of the poet, " were pure as pure could be."

CHAPTER VIII

A SUMMER IN GALLOWAY

" O bonnie hills of Galloway !   Oft have I stood to see,
  At sunset hour, your shadows fall, all darkening on the sea ;
  While visions of the buried years come o'er me in their might—
  As phantoms of the sepulchre—instinct with inward light."

THE spring of 1843 found me in Galloway, the land, once, of " the wild Scots."   I had been engaged by a son of the fine old patriarch of Parkhead, Fenwick, to go as tile-burner to him at the tileworks then on the farm of Broughton Mains, in the parish of Whithorn, and within some two miles of the beautiful little seaport town of Garlieston. Taking the old Victoria coach at Kilmarnock, which ran by way of Ayr, Maybole, Girvan, and Barrhill, on to Newton-Stewart, where I had to stay over night, I next morning got another coach to Garlieston, and from thence, with a large carpet bag in hand, I soon found my way to the dwelling at the works of my master, Mr Robert Picken, in whose household I was to stay.   My duties were to assist at the emptying and filling of the kiln on the Mondays and Tuesdays, and then to burn it off, which I generally succeeded in doing on the Friday mornings, having had to be in constant and sleepless attendance on it—sweating and sweltering over the fires, sixteen in number, during the previous two days and nights.   I had the rest of the week to myself, however, and might do what, or go where, I pleased, and though I had been without sleep, and toiling sore, without intermission, for so long a time, I never once thought of going to bed till the Friday night, and when not reading, I spent the two last days of the week in rambling about the beautiful country by wood and wild, on sounding shore and on mountain height, or in exploring " some old ruined castle grey," or some roofless and deserted fane of our early Christian forefathers, or in searching out the graves of the Martyrs of the Covenant, for whom and for their heroic struggles I had even then the most intense admiration. Sabbath I always spent at church, very unlike the working classes in that part of Wigtownshire, then at least. The great Disruption in the Church of Scotland, and which so shattered that ancient institution, was just about to take place when I arrived at Broughton Mains, and lecturers were everywhere going about rousing and instructing the people on the " Non-Intrusion " question. Two of these I heard speak in the Independent Church at Garlieston soon after my arrival—a Rev. Mr Duncan of Kirkintilloch and a Rev. Mr M'Gillvary (I forget from where); the first the most racy and brilliant lecturer I ever listened to, and whose admirable lectures tended greatly to make the people follow their ministers when, for conscience' sake, they so nobly left their churches and manses in the following month of May. Although I attended the Reformed Presbyterian Church at Whithorn, and the ministrations there of the Rev. Thomas M'Indoe, on nearly all other occasions, yet on the first Sabbath after the Disruption I went to the services of the Free Church party at Sorbie, where the assistant minister—the Rev. Mr Forrester—left the senior minister—the Rev. Mr Davidson—also his own father-in-law, behind, and took by far the greater part of the flock with him. It was also the Sacramental Sabbath, the Communion being partaken of in some school or hall, I forget which—short sermons being at the same time preached by several other ministers in a field close by; and hardly, if ever, have I heard such fervid or impassioned eloquence, or listened to such rapt and earnest prayers. The people, too, seemed equally earnest and equally inspired; and when I saw and thought of the high-handed action of the State in connection with the Stewarton and Strathbogie Church disputes, I remembered these fine, forcible lines in " The Poetic Mirror " of the Ettrick Shepherd (which I had just then been reading) when referring to the previous Martyrs of the Covenant :—

> " Tyrants ! could not misfortune teach
> That man has rights beyond your reach ?
> Thought ye the torture and the stake
> Could that intrepid spirit break,
> Which even in woman's breast withstood
> The terrors of the fire and flood ? "

The reference to the " flood " in these lines is evidently to the drowning at Wigtown of the aged widow of sixty and the maiden of only eighteen years, for their adherence to the covenanted work of Reformation, and which took place one hundred and fifty-eight years before the Disruption, and my first visit to Galloway. Having gone to Wigtown one Saturday in the summer of that year (1843) to pay brick duty—6s. 2d. of duty had then, and for years after, to be paid on every thousand of bricks made—one of the first places I sought out after having done my business was those humble martyrs' graves, and for that purpose I hied me to the old churchyard, not doubting but that the tombstones, which I knew had been set up at their graves, would be easily found. In this, however, I was mistaken. My search being vain—I could not find them; and as my experiences in my search were exactly those of that noble and exalted poetess, Mrs A. Stewart Monteath, as recorded by her in her " Lays of the Kirk and Covenant," as written some seven years later in a note to these lines—

> " A grave ! a grave is by the sea, in place of ancient tombs,
> A restless murmuring of the waves for ever o'er it comes,"

I give here her description of the place and of her search for the graves as so much better and more beautiful than anything I could pen.

" The small graveyard that surrounds the old church of Wigtown is a spot as attractive in its situation as interesting from the associations with which several of the time-worn tombstones are connected. So close to the shore that the sparkling waters on a summer's day seem, from a little distance, to kiss the monuments, there is incessant and inextricable mingling of the wind-voices and wave-voices within it suggestive of a thousand dreamy imaginations, and whispering of leaves and blossoms to the waters, and an answering again of waters to the leaves and blossoms, as though youth and life were breathing out their secrets and receiving in return the solemn confidence of death.

"It was a lovely day in autumn when I first stood within the precincts of that quiet churchyard. Our quest was for the graves of the martyrs, Margaret Wilson, whose eighteen summers had sufficed for acquiring the best of all wisdom, the wisdom that cometh from above, and her aged companion in the faith and patience of the Gospel, Margaret Maclachlan, of whom it is affectingly recorded that ' she was taken off her knees in prayer, and in her own house,' to be carried to prison and to death, and for some time we feared our search would be in vain. Having scrambled over a small dyke, from which the stones in many places had fallen partially, we found ourselves in a very wilderness of flowering weeds and the rankest vegetation, from amongst which the rude grey stones peeped up at intervals, apparently much in need of the timely intervention of some ' Old Mortality ' to preserve not only their inscriptions in their integrity but their very substance from decay. We groped about for a while in our uncertainty, clearing the tall grass first from one crumbling monument, then from another, laboriously spelling out superscriptions which proved to be not what we quested for, and at length had almost given up the venture in despair, when, having somehow guessed our dilemma, a tiny sun-burned urchin of a child came suddenly to our relief. Diving through weeds which truly reached above his middle, he guided us with unerring certainty to one of the least apparent gravestones, and bending down over it, with a childlike reverence in his features as he pointed to the scarcely legible inscription, he said, ' Look! she was but a lassie, yet she dee'd for the Covenant!' Very early in life I had listened to the story of the cruel and unheard-of wrong of those humble martyrs long before, from the lips of my devout, Covenanting father, and I cannot describe the mingled thrill of sorrow and of indignation which came over me when on that summer day I stood at

F

their graves in the quiet churchyard of that quietest of county towns."

Hardly less was I interested—though in a somewhat different way—with ruins, though small in size, of what is supposed to have been the first Christian church or place of worship in Scotland—that of St Ninian or St Ringan, on the shore near to the isle of Whithorn. St Ninian is said to have been of royal blood, and to have been born somewhere near to where the ruins of his church stands so long ago as the middle of the fourth century, and to have laboured successfully for the conversion to the Christian faith of the Picts of Galloway; and often there, and standing on the bold, precipitous, cave-pierced promontory of Borough Head on a calm and lovely summer night gazing across the deep blue sea, with the Isle of Man directly in front in the distance, I have had strange visions of the past; and nothing more terrible have I ever witnessed than a storm there, and on the bald rocky steep on which the ruins of Crugleton Castle stand, when the thundering waves beat upon the black, beetling cliffs, making the very rock-bound coast to tremble beneath my feet, the waves being churned into vast masses of foam which the wind caught up and bore far inland like flocks of birds filling the air. Near to the ruined castle, but still nearer to the fine mansion of the Earl of Galloway, there was then also the ruins of a small church, standing in the midst of a little-used burying ground, which having entered one night at the gloaming on my return from one of my rambles along the shore I was suddenly nearly startled out of my seven senses; for when wading among the long, rank grass, either some cast-up skull or a large shell upon which I had trampled gave a loud crack, and at the same moment an owl on or in a hole of the ruined wall gave a loud and an eldritch shriek which made me leap from that ancient place of graves with the agility of a wild deer, my heart at the same time beating against my ribs with the force almost of a well-handled hammer, though I soon came to myself on learning what at least the hideous cry was. The shore near to Galloway House is flat but beautiful, with the trees growing so near to the sea that at full-tide their branches, then, at least, almost dipped into the waves as they came curling and wantoning up to the shore. One day I met the then Earl of Galloway there, whom I did not know. As on these occasions I always took care to go well dressed, he touched his hat to me in return to my salute, looked at me, turned on his step, and spoke; and learning that it was Lord Galloway who was before me, I expressed the hope that I was committing no serious offence by being there. Discovering from my speech, I suppose, that I was from Ayrshire, and in reply to a question or two, my love of Nature and of scenery, he bade me come and walk through the policies as often as I chose, and learning my name, I was to tell any one who challenged me, that I had his permission, which they could learn from him. I, of course, thanked him for the privilege, and to this day think kindly of the good earl, long now sleeping with his fathers.

When here—in Galloway—I read with the most exquisite delight, the poems, essays, and " Citizen of the World," of dear, simple, kind, and amiable Oliver Goldsmith, and the very different poems of Byron, and other works of the kind; and amongst the religious works which also delighted me were the sermons of John Logan, many of which are really eloquent, and I have often felt sorry since that I ever afterwards discovered the meanness of his conduct to his deceased friend, Michael Bruce, the best of whose poems (and I have fully looked into the case) he stole, beyond any reasonable or honest doubt, and published as his own.

In the early autumn of this year I was the certain means of saving the life of a sprightly, rather pretty, and a most amiable and intelligent young lady, the daughter of a neighbouring farmer. I was taking a walk, all by myself, one lovely night, along a narrow by-road, reading, as I slowly walked along, Southey's stately but heavy eastern poem, " The Curse of Kehama," and was standing transfixed and amazed at the truth and beauty of these lofty lines in the 10th Canto—the finest, perhaps, on the subject in the language—on the immortality of love, beginning with the lines—

"They sin who tell us love can die.
    With life all other passions fly,
        All others are but vanity,"

when I was roused from my musing by the loud rattle of
wheels and the sound of horse's feet galloping towards me
at no great distance, and near to me a young woman
running distractedly in my direction screaming, for on
either side there was a pretty high stone fence, over which,
in trying to get out of the way of the runaway horse, she
fell, at the same time uttering a piercing scream. In a
moment I comprehended the situation and the danger both
to her and to myself, and thrusting the volume into my
pocket, I was instantly at her side, and catching hold of
her I lifted her up and in a manner threw her over the
dyke, and vaulting over it myself had not a moment to
spare when the animal came rushing past us, upsetting
the cart and falling itself a little way beyond in trying
to make in at a gate that led off the narrow road into
a field. The young lady was so excited that it was some
time before she could express her thanks to me for—as
she said—saving her life. In assisting her home, we were
met by her father, who had seen my action from the house,
and he so warmly thanked me also for what I had done
that I almost began to think myself a hero, especially
when the lady-like mother loaded me with thanks and
praise with tear-filled eyes and a voice trembling with
emotion. What pleased me most, however, was the oft-
repeated thanks and praise of the young lady herself, as
she afterwards called very often on Mrs Picken, with
whom I stayed, and with whom she had become acquainted. On these occasions she offered me books on
loan, the merits of which we discussed together for
periods of considerable length, and which began to grow
longer and longer though always seeming to be shorter;
and I fear we would have fallen in love with each other
had I not left the place at the end of the season and
returned again to my native Ayrshire, for she began to
see ever new beauties in the love-lyrics of Burns, Moore,
and Tannahill, and I also began to see poetry in her very

step and to hear the most agreeable music in her voice.
How changed she must be now if she is still in the land
of the living !

> " O Woman ! woman ! ever true and kind,
>   Thou sweet perfection of the gentle mind ;
>   Bless'd to refine thy lord-like brother-man—
>   The last, but loveliest, of the Almighty plan."

CHAPTER IX

A HOME AMONG THE HILLS

"But on and up, where Nature's heart
Beats strong amid the hills."
RICHARD MONCKTON MILNES.

By the merest chance (if there be such a thing as chance as it is commonly understood) I was engaged to go to the hill country of New Cumnock in the spring of 1844. A young friend and neighbour, going thither to visit some relatives with whom I was also acquainted, turned back, after he was past my father's house, for the purpose of getting me to go with him, and after a good deal of persuasion I went without the least thought of any engagement, but was engaged nevertheless to go to the son-in-law of my former master, Mr Boyd, as tile burner and assistant manager; and the simple incident of that young man calling upon me was the cause of my going to the Cumnock district, where I have now spent more than sixty years of my not uneventful life.

My new master, Hugh Meikle, was the younger son of a small landed proprietor in the Irvine valley about half-way between Galston and Newmilns, and had been well brought up. He was a man of excellent principles, and, though not very brilliant intellectually, yet fairly well read, with some taste for literature. He was an excellent master, kind, considerate, and obliging, and as he made me very much of a companion, the period of between three and four years I was with him was a very happy one, and my duties being very much the same as those I had to perform in Galloway, I had always the two last days of the week to do as I liked or go where I pleased; and as, in the near vicinity, there were many places both of beauty and of interest, these I soon made myself acquainted with—from the highest mountain tops to the most secluded valleys; tracing the streams that ran among the hills, treading the woods and traversing the moors—the latter being one of my principal delights, especially in brown autumn, when the untrodden wastes were all ablaze with the blooming heather, amid which myriads of "busy bees" kept up an unceasing hum from early dawn until the lengthening shadows vanished from the desert wilds, and the daylight had died away upon the western clouds.

Long previous to this I had, in the language of Alexander Pope, "lisped in numbers, for the numbers came," but few of these effusions I preserved, and coming, as they did, easily, perhaps they were not worth preserving, for Sheridan at least, in his own wicked way, has said that "easy writing is mostly d——d hard reading." Now, however, I took courage to send one of my pieces to the *Ayr Advertiser*, which the late Mr Thomas M. Gemmell, the proprietor and editor of that old and well-conducted paper, published, and not only did so, but wrote me some encouraging words when I sent him a second poem, which he also published. I still entertain a warm regard for his memory because of his kind encouragement of me; and because the *Advertiser* was the first paper in which I ever appeared in print I have a warm side to that excellent paper still. The first poem was entitled "The Storm," and it is not deficient in descriptive power, but as William Nicholson, the Galloway poet, said of his inimitable poem "The Brownie of Blednoch," "it has one great defect—it wants a moral."

In 1846 I published a small volume of poems with the title of "The Hermit of Westmoreland, The Covenanter's Revenge, and other poems," which met with a better reception than I now think it deserved; for while, here and there, there are, I feel sure enough, some passages of true poetry, yet as a whole it is very unequal, and I am now so very much ashamed of it that could I gather in every copy of it still in existence I would commit them all to the flames. In one of the poems, however—that of

"The Deserted Castle"—there are some just and vigorous lines on the cruel wrongs which the amiable and talented Lady Flora Hastings was subjected to, and which bore her down to an untimely grave of a broken heart.

Two years before that time I had begun to write for *The Kilmarnock Journal*, an ultra-Tory paper, then edited and at last partly owned by the publisher, Mr Matthew Wilson, a man of considerable shrewdness. The paper even then was dying of sheer weakness, although with but a very small circulation it kept on in existence for some years after I began to send occasional small contributions to its columns.

Having become tacksman of the works, I in 1851 paid a ten days' visit to the great London Exhibition of that year, visiting also one of the dear lads of Windyhill— Mr John Boyd—then at Gosport, and with him visiting also the Isle of Wight. When in London on a Sunday I heard the late Rev. Dr Cumming preach, who was then at the height of his fame, both as a preacher and as a religious author, and some of his works (whatever may be thought of his prophetic writings) ought not to be forgotten, his "Voices of the Night" especially, which is as eloquently written as it is fervently and devoutly pious. I also heard a man of far greater power and genius when there—the late Dr Croly, rector of St Stephen's, Walbrook, author of the greatest and most magnificent of all eastern romances—"Salathiel," and many other works in both prose and poetry. He had been giving a series of sermons on the Ten Commandments, and his discourse that day was on that very delicate one, the seventh, and only a man of great judgment, culture, ability, and genius could have handled the theme so as not to bring a blush into any woman's face in the church. In London I visited the great sights—St Paul's and Westminster Cathedrals. The latter interested me by far the most, and in the Poet's Corner I lingered long and could have remained far longer had my time permitted; and the same was also the case when I visited the British Museum, and particularly when among the Egyptian and Assyrian mummies, paintings, and sculptures. The year before this my father died, as I have already related, and while away I wrote daily to my aged mother, now a lonely widow. My eldest brother, John—the eldest of the second family of my father—died ten weeks after him, and having been in bad health for a length of time and not able, properly, to attend to his tileworks, limeworks, and the farm which he had also taken, I suffered by his death to the extent of fully £200, and for doing so, though in silence, instead of receiving thanks, I also endured not a little unjust obloquy. About the same time I had been induced to become a partner with a brother-in-law in extensive brick and tile works at Dalquharran, on the beautiful water of Girvan. He was out of a situation, and unless I had become joint tenant with him in the works, the factor (the late Mr Wm. Brown, solicitor, Maybole) would not let the works to him alone. I had also to bind myself to ride or drive through weekly (there was no railway to the place then) to see how things were going at the works. By the way of Dal-mellington and Straiton it was, going and coming, a ride of fifty miles, or going by Ayr and Maybole the distance was seventy miles; and that distance my fleet, beautiful, and docile grey mare "Brenda" often carried me in the saddle without the least fatigue. My brother-in-law was a man of skill, honest, intelligent, and upright; but he took snuff, and had a habit of telling long and interminable stories to the workers, with snuff-box in hand, and keeping them (nearly fifty in number) standing listening and idle, very often at the dinner and breakfast hours, for fifteen or twenty minutes past the hour—the result of which was that for the year there was a direct loss of fully £64, besides my loss of time and expense in riding through, which I had to bear, for he, good, honest man, had not a penny to meet it.

"Misfortunes," it has been well and long said, "never come singly," and so having been urged to allow a younger brother to go and start a new tilework in the Island of Bute, and as he had to give long credit to his customers, and the machinery which had been put into the work by the proprietor was very incomplete, and the clayfield then with no proper fall for the water, the business was a losing one; and having been induced to become a party on a cash credit for several hundred pounds by some Bute farmers, who wrote me they were going to be co-obligants on the deed, though they afterwards in the most wonderful way refused to sign it unless I would grant them a back letter relieving them of liability, I soon found myself involved to the full extent, and for very considerable other sums to keep the cash credit square. My own work still paying well I still, however, struggled on, being young, sanguine, and not without energy and skill in business. My brother, who could no more help himself than he had any *intention* of injuring me, afterwards went abroad, settling, or rather *unsettling*, in Canada; for he and his family flitted fourteen times in the course of five years; and they becoming sick of the country, as well as sick from ague, I, at his earnest and repeated solicitations, paid £35 to a Shipping Company in Glasgow to bring them over; furnishing a house for them and meeting them at and bringing them out from Glasgow. Since then, and years and years ago, they have gone to New Zealand, and he is now, with his large family, doing a big business as a sewage pipe and brick and tile manufacturer there, and he may yet, and soon, remember "Joseph" and not forget him.

In the book of Job we are told that "great men are not always wise," and so neither are ordinary mortals like myself. Not very cautious or wise, therefore, as will thus be seen, in business matters, I was just as little so in some literary ones—and it is just as well to make confession of these things here, and to the public, instead of privately to a priest.

In 1853 I was foolish enough to be wheedled into writing a satirical poem called "The Interdict," in which a minister of the Edinburgh Presbytery got his colleague, most of his session, and even his precentor somewhat mercilessly lashed, in verse, parts of which, after quoting the whole, the Edinburgh newspapers declared to be perfectly Miltonic in power. The whole poem certainly was so at least in daring, for Satan himself is one of the interlocutors in it. The satire caused the *inspirer* of it to be libelled by the Edinburgh Presbytery, the case occupying the attention of that venerable Court for several months, and ended in the acquittal of their " brother," although he is believed to have previously confessed his guilt to the rev. D.D. who led the defence ! So much was I blamed in the matter that I was forced to publish a pamphlet in my own defence, in which the doubtful doings of the majority of the Presbytery were laid bare and shown in such a curious light that, as the late Rev. Dr Rankine of Sorn once said to me, those of them who had read it once never dared to look into it again.

While residing at Wellhill tileworks I was a member of one large debating society of very varied talent, and afterwards of a literary society, the members of which were not numerous, but all were men of high principles and of considerable culture and ability. But few members of either are now alive, and of the latter society I now know of only two, including myself, who are still in the land of the living, while the other, and the youngest member of the society, and one of the most able and excellent, is so deaf that he could hardly hear it though " heaven's last thunder " was to roll along the sky to-morrow. Thanks to a good God, though the poorest of them all, in as far as worldly wealth is concerned, I am still strong and well, and am writing these lines without the aid of glasses.

In 1861, as I have already related, my dear mother died, which was the sorest blow I ever had or have ever got. Two years later the tileworks—where I had lived for eighteen years—and the farm near to it, which my brother's widow gave up to me, were taken from me through a person then on the estate cruelly misrepresenting me to Lord Bute's factor. I had previously built a large new kiln, and erected new pan rollers and other machinery, at a cost of over £350, at the tileworks; while at the farm I had drained thirty acres, and built a whole steading of office houses without the least help from the landlord, and there being then no law by which a tenant could claim for improvements I lost the whole.

More than this, although every out-going tenant gets paid for his grass seeds, and the in-coming tenant would have paid me for it, the then land steward would not allow him, though not a sheep nor a hoof had been pastured upon it. And although there was hardly a fence on the farm when my brother got it, I was forced to put these and the gates into the best condition when I left it. O, the injustice of spiteful men! I wonder if such a man dared ever utter the prayer, "The Universal Prayer," of Alexander Pope, the Catholic poet—

> "Such mercy I to others show,
> Like mercy show to me."

I did not blame the Marquis of Bute for this, for he was then a minor; nor did I blame his tutors-at-law in any great degree, for they would act just according to the representations made to them—or rather to the one tutor-at-law, Sir James Fergusson, then residing at Dumfries House—though as I had not only supported him with my vote, but with my ever ready and active pen, at every Parliamentary election, and have still beside me his holograph letters thanking me, he might, I thought then and think still, have at least heard me and allowed me to state my case and to plead my cause before him personally, especially when I did not owe the landlord a penny of rent. It was the influence brought to bear upon the factor against me, that was the cause of the whole. The person I refer to from the first took deep umbrage at me, and became jealous of me because that once in his presence the late Mr David Shaw, then Lord Bute's factor, a most upright and excellent man, consulted me and took my advice as to the prices he should pay for the making of the various sizes of drain tiles at one of the estate tile-works near to the village of Ochiltree. My clear-headed mother saw what was brewing before she died, in the long consultations my traducer had with one whom I trusted at the works when I happened to be from home; and she once said to me regarding the foreman that "something would be seen on that false creature yet that would appal people"; while of the other she said, in the words of the patriarch

Job : " Men shall clap their hands at him and shall hiss him out of his place." Luther once said that he would rather have a whole army of men against him than the prayers of one Christian man or woman; and however these men (long since gone to their account) might be affected by my Christian mother's prayers, it is a fact that the first died many years ago in the Island of Bute, after a long illness, " a terror unto himself and to all around him "; and the other, when big with self-importance, and dreading and suspecting nothing, was summarily dismissed, and spent his remaining years in unhonoured obscurity and hopping about on crutches! " Verily," as the Psalmist says, " there is a God to judge upon the earth." For what I expended on the tileworks and farm and had to leave behind me, Lord Bute (who was blameless) was not a penny the richer, and indeed knew nothing of it; and were those who were the real instruments of it ever any the happier? I trow not; and although I may be much the poorer, I have a store of good health and a buoyancy of spirits which the richest might envy.

CHAPTER X

FROM THE COUNTRY TO THE TOWN

" Let those who are in favour with their stars,
Of public honours and proud titles boast,
Whilst I, whom fortune of such triumph bars,
Unlook'd for joy in that I honour most."
WILLIAM SHAKESPEARE.

WHILST at Wellhill tileworks a sad accident occurred to one of my best workmen, by which he lost his life, and of which, strange to say, I had an undoubted premonition in a dream; and not only had I this, but the unfortunate man himself had a like warning, for, mystery of mysteries! he had exactly the same dream as myself, and also at the same time, the very night before, which has long made me a believer in what the great German dramatist, Frederick Schiller, says in " The Robbers," that " dreams come from God," some of them at least. In my dream—which troubled me all through the night—I thought I was in a deep, dark, and exceedingly lonesome valley, where great, gloomy trees almost excluded the light, and between the rocky banks of which ran a black, sluggish stream. This man, I thought, was my sole companion, and though there was no bridge and no way to get to the other side, cross it he said he must; then, uttering a loud cry of terror, before I could look round he was out of sight; but where he had vanished to, or how, I could not divine, for the stream still, I thought, flowed slowly on, smooth and unruffled, and neither upon the near nor the farther bank could he be seen, although not a moment before he had been at my side. The dream made me uneasy—everything connected with it being so dismal and dreary and so very distinct; but I said nothing of it until, when the men were eating their dinners in the engine-house, I entered and saw the companion of my dream sitting in a corner by himself, to

94

whom I said that I had had a strange dream about him the previous night; when he said that he had been equally troubled by a dream, in which he and I were the only actors, and on being asked, he told me his dream, which, to my great consternation, I found was—both as to place and incidents—exactly my dream, only that he said he had found himself in a moment snatched off and beneath the stream, when uttering, as he thought, a piercing cry he awoke. Musing with much surprise on what such a strange coincidence might mean, I went down to my dwelling-house, some seventy yards away, and had hardly begun to partake of my own dinner when a boy came running in with a cry that James M'Culloch was 'killed. Running up I found that on starting the engine, he had found the key of a small iron shaft, which ran along the joists and which drove the pipe-tile machine, loose, and that, without stopping the engine, he had climbed up to drive it tight, and in stooping to do so a strong silk napkin that he wore round his neck had been caught by the machinery, when he was whirled several times round the shaft. At first I thought there was not much wrong, for he was able, by leaning upon my arm, to walk down to the house, saying as he walked—"This is my dream, it's a' up wi' me"; and though a doctor was brought with all possible speed, he sank and died from internal bleeding in less than three hours after the accident. These are truths in every particular, and the wisest men among us cannot account for such a double dream in two individuals, and on the same night, and with the sad result which followed, let them "argue and discuss, reason and disclose," as long as they may; although numbers, with no more knowledge than their fellows, will laugh at the mysterious circumstance and talk glibly and sneeringly about "superstition." although they may be, and indeed are, unable to show that, in many matters connected with human existence, there are not many times some direct agency of a superior power in such extraordinary events as these.

Dog stories are numerous: let me give one or two. I had two dogs at the tileworks, one a beautiful brown water dog, which always attended and waited upon my father wherever he went. An old man, a farmer in the district, used often to visit my father, and one day, when conveying him part of the way home, they sat down at the side of a wood, just out of sight of the house, and having sat so long on the grass their limbs grew so stiff that when essaying to rise, they found that neither of them could do so, and after struggling for a time the thought struck my father to call in the aid of Oscar, the dog, who, having been standing looking on, comprehended the case at once; so holding out the end of his staff to the sturdy little dog, he told him to catch hold of it and pull, which he did with all his might. My father, holding the other end with one hand and raising himself with the other hand, at once succeeded in getting up, when he assisted to set his brother in tribulation also upon his legs.

My other dog was one of great size, a breed between a Spanish wolf dog and a Newfoundland, jet black and as wise as a man, and knowing not only every word I spoke to him, but, in a manner, my very thoughts; for if I was troubled (my looks doubtless showing it), he was dull and troubled too; while if I was cheerful, he too was frolicsome and happy. He had a terrible temper, and was very ferocious, but I had him fully under command. Keeping him always chained during the day, and also at night, but always giving him a walk myself every morning, and generally also at night, he minded nobody unless they began to make of him and praise him (which, like his master, he did not relish) when he would growl and look dangerous. Once, however, he had almost devoured one of my workmen who one day left off work because of some little quarrel about some matter of small importance, and as he was leaving said some most irritating thing to me and then took to his heels. I was so nettled at his insolence that I made after him and caught him a little way beyond and in sight of where the dog was chained, and though he struggled with me I made him spin back before me, when he not only began to his work again, but returned to it next morning in the grey dawn, and just as I was giving "Captain" his morning walk. The dog was some thirty yards from me at the time, and though he had barked wildly and strained at the chain the day before when I drove the runaway man back before me, I never dreamed that he would mind the man afterward; but, designing, doubtless, to punish him then for what he had seen the day before, the instant he caught sight of the fellow he sprang upon him with a terrific roar and drove him to the ground and made to worry poor Samuel Reid, who uttered a yell of terror which rang through the works. Comprehending the matter in a moment, I also cried loudly in turn; and as I had the ferocious animal entirely under control, he desisted instantly; but poor Reid did not cease crying and trembling till nearly midday; and good cause he had to be afraid, for so strong was the dog's jaws that I once saw him crush and devour the boiled head of a blackfaced sheep—swallowing the whole in twenty-five minutes! When he had reached the age of thirteen years I had to destroy him for one day attacking my mother when she was feeding him. So ferocious was he known to be that before two men, with guns each, would venture to approach and shoot him, I had to tie him to a tree, when, possessed—as he all along had been—of the wisdom and knowledge of a human being, he most certainly comprehended the awful and immediate fate which awaited him, for the pitiful, pleading look he gave, followed by a howl of anguish and terror as I began to move away from him, seem to rise up before me at this distant day. I made his grave in a lone, secluded, though rather pretty spot, which not very long since I walked a good distance to visit, and not without emotion stood beside it for a considerable time, thinking of the changes which had passed over myself and the dwellers of that countryside since then.

Cats, though much less intelligent than dogs, often, however, do very wonderful things; and I will relate at least one strange cat story here. Having possession of the farm (that of Taiglem, Cumnock) for six months after I had to leave the tileworks, I removed to it at Martinmas, 1862, and had to leave a black-and-white cat behind me, it running off to and among the tile sheds, so that we could not get a hold of it when flitting down to the farm, which

G

is quite a mile distant. It is nothing unusual for cats to return great distances to places from which they have been taken; but next day this cat followed us to the farm, though it is quite out of sight of the tileworks, and how it had found us out passes my comprehension.

About the year 1850 I had a visit paid me by a Mr John Davidson Browne, known as "The Bard of Glazert," from a volume of poems with that title which he had published in 1845. I was ignorant of both the man and his book until he came and introduced himself one day and presented me with a copy of the poems, in which there really is some more than creditable poetry, particularly one poem, "To my Native Land," written in America, and consisting of fully one hundred lines, and which is truly excellent both in feeling and expression. The man, however, who had been a schoolmaster, was a fool and very unsteady, and after prolonging his visit for two or three days I was glad to see his back and to hear the sound of his departing footsteps. He had brought with him a second volume of "Ballads connected with Ayrshire Traditions." These mostly are really spirited and excellent; and as the great northern critic, the Rev. George Gilfillan, was then writing largely for "Hogg's Instructor" and giving monthly criticisms of "Bundles of Books"—in which, minister of the Gospel though he was, he would tell us that during the previous month alone he had *read and critically examined* from 200 to 300 volumes—Mr Browne determined on sending his new volume to the reverend critic, and after a good deal of persuasion got me to send him my maiden volume also; and notice them he did, and in his own inflated, big, bombastic, earthquake-rumbling style gave both volumes a thorough slating. I laughed, but had not learned then, nor have I learned yet, the Christian meekness and submission of, when struck on the one cheek, turning the other also to the smiter, and so I replied with some spirit in the columns of the *Ayr Advertiser*, and succeeded in making Mr Gilfillan look very ridiculous at the least. He was honest and forgiving enough to notice my next work—"Poems, Lectures, and Miscellanies"—most favourably, and at considerable length. The criticism, however, drove " The Bard of Glazert " frantic and he came to me again, when I tried to cheer him up and disregard the critique, and gave him two pounds to lift part of his little publication from his printer and deliver copies to his subscribers, when he would be able to get a greater number, but from that day to this I have never seen nor heard of him, further than that he had got on the *fuddle* and thus spent the money I gave him, and then all trace of him was lost. It is believed that he had managed to get back to America, where, too, likely his bones rest in an unknown grave. In the third volume of " Edward's Modern Scottish Poets," 1881, will be found a sketch of the career of this wayward son of song which—with many other sketches—I wrote for that work. There also readers will find specimens of his poetry, the worst of which, however, is better than the best passage in Mr George Gilfillan's dull, heavy, dismal poem on " Night," by which, in his swaggering and ambitious style, he meant to put Milton's self into the shade. Both poet and poem being now, however, dead and buried—the last without any hope of a resurrection—let me in charity " speak gently of the dead."

I cannot help also mentioning here that for some years during the lifetime of my parents there resided with us at the tileworks a fine young lad, whose after success in life was undoubtedly very largely due to the knowledge of the Bible imparted to him by my venerable father, and to the love and reverence for it, and for true religion which he acquired under our roof. Going out to Australia in the fifties, Hugh Harris (that is his name) has long since become a large and prosperous farmer, a magistrate, a mature Christian, a credit to the old country and a great acquisition to the new.

> " From scenes like these old Scotia's grandeur springs,
>   That makes her loved at home, revered abroad."

At Whitsunday, 1863, I removed to Afton-Bridgend, New Cumnock, without knowing very well how to shape my course for the future, and having felt my home unspeakably dull since the death of my dear mother, and feeling the need also I had of someone to take an interest in and manage my household, I thought my best course would be to marry, being then forty-one years of age, and which I did in the June of that year, choosing as my wife the sister of him who had lost his life in so melancholy a manner at the tilework and a great-grand-niece of Dr Alexander Murray, Professor of Oriental Languages in the University of Edinburgh, and thus on the mother's side and on till her own day, sprung from a long race of Galloway shepherds; and though not gifted in the Aryan languages like that wonderful scholar, she is a linguist too, in a way! Of her, however, I can truly say as Lord Beaconsfield said of his wife—she is " the most severe of critics, but the best of wives."

For the following six months, save engaging in some harvest work, I was without any particular calling, and spent much of my time during the long summer days in rambling through the classic and beautiful Afton valley, tracing this most pellucid of streams to its source, climbing the highest hills which rise amid that great mountain range which separates Ayrshire from Galloway, and in reading largely. At Martinmas I removed into the more stirring and business town of Old Cumnock, in which I have ever since resided, and where my literary career really began.

CHAPTER XI

THE TOWN AND THE NEWSPAPER

"God made the country and man made the town."
WILLIAM COWPER.

"Here shall the Press the people's rights maintain,
Unawed by influence and unbribed by gain;
Here patriot truth her glorious precepts draw,
Pledged to Religion, Liberty, and Law."
JOSEPH STORY.

ALTHOUGH to people who have been all their lives used to the crowded streets, the hurry, rush, and roar of a great commercial city such as Glasgow, the town of Old Cumnock with less than four thousand inhabitants, with one stream passing through it, and with another, and a larger one—the Lugar—half surrounding it, with green hills and waving woods seen from almost every street and alley in it, would be looked upon as quiet and altogether the country—still, to me, who had been born, brought up, and always had my dwelling where there existed only a single habitation, and where dwelt but a single family, even the smart, airy little town of Old Cumnock looked quite a city. Not only also had my delight been to reside in such "quiet habitations," but always whenever opportunity presented itself I had a longing desire to be off and away, and generally alone, to the desert wilds or to the solemn-looking hills, where, save "the whistling of plover and bleating of sheep," with the sound of the tinkling rills which stray among the mountain valleys, when in the glad green months of spring, of buxom summer, or of rich and mellow autumn, "my converse was with heaven alone," through the medium of Nature. And when I remembered, too, that the builder of the first city (Cain) was a murderer, I also remembered how numerous were the great events in

the world's history which had been transacted on high hills
and among the mountain solitudes, and these have ever
given me a wonderful love for the mountains and the hills,
which America's still best and most genial author, Washington Irving, so happily designates as

> " Nature's strong-built battlements,
> The masonry of God."

I often thought that it was in no building made with
hands that God delivered His law to Moses (that law by
which the affairs of all civilised nations still are guided),
but on the bold, lonely heights of Horeb ; that it was on
the still more secluded heights of Mount Hor that Aaron,
the first and greatest high priest of Israel, yielded up his
breath ; and that it was on Mount Nebo and from the
top of Pisgah that his still greater brother viewed the
Promised Land, and then died, and had the most marvellous burial on record, being buried by the Lord ! The
life of the future King of Israel—David—is never more
interesting than when he is skipping about on the hill of
Hachilah, and hiding in the cave of Adullum. Often had
I mused on the simple and uncorrupted Christians of
Piedmont and the valleys of the Valois, who refused to
submit to the authority of the Pope of Rome, defying his
edicts and finding shelter from the bloody and exterminat-
ing sword of his minions among the sublime rocky fast-
nesses which frown high over the dashing and foaming
waters of the Po, the Sturia, the Tanaro, and their tribu-
taries. Often, too, had I traversed the broad moors and
climbed the high hills in our own northern land of mist and
wind to which our own Covenanting heroes betook themselves, in the evil times when the two last cruel and
infatuated Stuart Kings ruled the land where Richard
Cameron thundered against " the rulers of that iron time,"
and where the *weird* old Alexander Peden lurked and
prayed when the folds of the misty cloud would hide him
so miraculously from his pursuers. To me, therefore, the
voice of the desert, and of the great mountain ranges of
our native land, was never dumb ; and to leave these
lonely haunts, with all their many and loved associations

for "the deavin', dinsome town" where, for the song of the lark, I would have that of some broken-winded, crack-voiced street singer ; and for the song of the thrush the harsh sound of a barrel-organ or some discordant hurdy-gurdy ; and for the smell of the fragrant hawthorn and the sweet-scented wild thyme I would have the sickening odour of a cesspool, or the pestilence-wooing smell of a row of foul ashpits ; and where for deep-thinkers among the people I would have the glib-tongued talkers, but men and women less given to silent meditation, was a change as great as it was dreaded. Thanks, however, to a country gentleman—the late Mr John Hyslop, of Bank, New Cumnock—one of the best men I have ever known, whose life and that of his son (the present laird of Bank and Afton, who follows well in his father's footsteps) I had previously been instrumental in saving one dark winter night when accidentally thrown out of their gig, I was ere long enabled to build a pretty cottage in the southern suburb of the town, where with a flower garden in front and a fruit and vegetable one behind, I can look out on green fields on every side, and where in the glorious summer and golden autumn time I can see the sun sinking behind the blue splintered peaks of Arran, his last crimson rays glowing among the tree-tops which crown the nearer heights like the burning bush of Horeb.

The old *Kilmarnock Journal* being by this time defunct, I acted for some time as correspondent for *The Ayr Advertiser*; and afterwards for *The Cumnock Express*, soon after it was started —now more than thirty years ago—when I was engaged to write for it, and of which I have long now had the charge here. Years previous to this, however, and long before it came into the hands of its present owner, Provost Ferguson, I had written frequently and not a little for *The Ayr Observer*, when contests were taking place for the representation of the county in Parliament, having been all my life mildly but firmly, consistently. and conscientiously Conservative, although for some years I also wrote (though non-politically) for *The Ayrshire Post*, in the columns of which I published two novels of the ordinary three-volume length each, with afterwards some smaller tales. One of these was meant to show the evils of the large farm system, by which the country districts were being depopulated, and the best part of our hardy and industrious peasantry driven to pine and sicken in the towns and to the overcrowding of these; or they were forced to seek for new homes in foreign lands, "friends, kindred, country to behold no more." In the inculcating of these opinions, of course, a good plot had to be constructed and love scenes introduced; and in all these the best judges thought and said I had succeeded.

In taking the conduct of the *Express*, which is a weekly paper, I saw at once that it was necessary to report local matters very fully and at much greater length than imperial affairs or foreign news, for these were being seen and read daily in the city newspapers. I found, too, that it was necessary to know something of almost every subject, and to be able to write upon it; and my large and desultory reading, with a pretty retentive memory, thus stood and stands me in excellent stead. Let those who may, rail at desultory reading, I know it has been of immense service to me. For many years now I have written a weekly agricultural article, generally of a column's length, for *The Ayr Observer* and *The Cumnock Express*, the one article serving for both papers; my having received both a practical and a scientific knowledge of agriculture, with the faculty of always keeping my eyes open to everything going on in the country around me, enables me to do so without "running to seed." To give these weekly articles a sort of unique interest I always head them with a poetical text appropriate to the subject to be discussed, and in which articles I have never troubled myself to chronicle the state of the markets either at home or abroad, knowing well that farmers now obtain these not weekly but daily from the city newspapers. During my time I have had many controversies in the papers, and while these were often not a little acrimonious, still I am not aware that I have ever made a real, a permanent or a spiteful enemy; not even Mr J. Keir Hardie, now M.P., whose pen, like the swords of the Ishmaelites, was generally (when writing for *The Cumnock News*) against every man, and always against myself; and who seemed to glory in getting a castigation, no matter how severe if it was the means of keeping him before the public, and so I found you might as well try to chastise a crocodile with a silk whip, as to make the clever, socialistic Mr Hardie wince by the most severe things that could be written of him!

Previous to the ballot being introduced at Parliamentary elections, the conduct of the rowdies was generally bad everywhere, and in no place was it worse, or perhaps so utterly bad as in the town of Old Cumnock, and it was like going through a campaign in an enemy's country for a Conservative to go to the poll and record his vote. On one occasion, in addition to the local police and special constables, thirty picked police constables were brought from Glasgow to keep the peace and protect " the Tories," who, generally, driven to the poll in carriages, and intending to return by them to the committee-rooms, were mostly unable to do so; for when attempting to enter the carriage they were driven by the number and weight of the mob past the carriage door in spite of all the police could do, when they were hustled into the Square, spit upon, pricked with awls, brogs, and nails; pinned up to the walls or to the Market Cross by the pressure of the roughs, and used in the most shameful fashion; more than one individual being knocked down and trampled upon and never being well afterwards, their deaths, beyond a doubt, being due to the dastardly conduct of those whom the late William Buchanan, at one time minister of the parish of Kilmaurs, then editor of *The Ayr Observer*, thus addressed :—

> " O ! rowdies of Old Cumnock,
>   Enlightened *Sans Cullotte*,
> With knives and nails for arguments,
>   To teach us how to vote ! "

As then very many householders were without votes, on account of the restricted state of the franchise, those who were thus shut out from having any voice in political matters doubtless felt that this was the only way they had of making their influence felt; and if they did not thereby succeed in doing so with the Government, they certainly managed to do so on the hips and hinder parts of the, to them, most obnoxious Tories. And not only by acting thus but by hustling them up to and tripping them upon stinking dunghills, and by using language towards them and heaping epithets upon them which might have "made the angels weep," if there be tears among the celestials.

Fully thirty years ago a strange circumstance happened to me, which I cannot refrain from relating here. Among the authors, poets, and others with whom I had become acquainted, one of the greatest as a poet, and best as a man, was the late Thomas Aird, of Dumfries, long editor of the *Dumfries Herald*, and the intimate friend of Carlyle, Professor Wilson, and, indeed, of most literary men of note of the first half of the last century, and who, as a poet of originality, sublimity, and power, ought to occupy one of the highest seats in the temple of Fame, for his poem entitled "The Devil's Dream" has not been excelled in lofty grandeur and weird, fascinating power since the "Paradise Lost" of Milton appeared. In the early spring of 1876 I knew that Mr Aird was ill, yet I had not heard anything of him, nor had he even been at all in my thoughts, till one bright and lovely evening in April, when taking a walk on a height overlooking the town, and when watching and admiring the setting sun far in the west shooting his long lines of rosy light in among the lofty peaks of Goatfell, the thought darted across my mind—How was Mr Aird keeping? and ere I was aware I found myself unconsciously repeating these exceedingly beautiful and touching lines in his noble tale of "Buy a Broom," in his prose volume, "The Old Bachelor," and which he puts into the mouth of the Italian boy bewailing the death of his sister; and thinking the lines — and indeed the whole poem — exceedingly beautiful, I found myself repeating them a second time :—

"Now, sailing by, the butterfly may through the lattice peer,
   To tell the prime of Summer time—the glory of the year;

But ne'er for me; to death her eyes have given up their trust,
And I cannot reach them in the grave, to clear them of the
dust.

" But in the skies her peerless eyes the mother-maid hath kiss'd,
And she hath dipp'd her sainted foot in the sunshine of the
bless'd.
Eternal peace her ashes keep! who lov'd me through the
past;
And may good Christ my spirit take to be with her's at last! "

Little did I know then that just in that very hour the
films of death were gathering over the eyes of Mr Aird,
and that they would glow no more here below with all
a poet's rapture and joy, as his were wont so often to do
while he gazed at day's decline upon the rich and glorious
saffron and orange tints which often, at the quiet sunset
hour, colour and make glorious the grand old granite
hills of Galloway. It struck me much when next day I
learned of Mr Aird's death, that he and his poetry and
his very appearance, as I saw him last in Dumfries, should
have come just then—at the very hour of his death—
so vividly into my mind. Although no man was more
beloved and respected in Dumfries than Mr Aird, yet he
lived too near to our own time for full justice to be done
to his genius and writings, and I could not but feel sad
when, now a good many years ago, at the inauguration of
the Burns statue at Dumfries, neither Lord Rosebery
nor Sheriff Nicholson, nor any of the speakers, had the
slightest reference to make to the exalted poet, the sincere
Christian, and the good man then but recently taken from
us. Perhaps they hardly knew of him or his noble
achievements in literature at all, for your real, and in this
respect half-insane, Scottish Burns worshippers know and
recognise hardly any poet save Coila's bard, whom they
place far above David, the poet King of Israel, " the
rapt Isaiah," or any poet of our country; although,
perhaps, had Burns, with all his genius, been living and
walking the earth to-day, and come asking a subscription
for his volume, many who now shout themselves hoarse
in his praise would have been more ready to hound their
dogs at him than grant his modest request.

CHAPTER XII

PILGRIMAGES TO POETIC PLACES

" Hie away! hie away!
  Over bank and over brae,
  Where the copse wood is the greenest,
  Where the fountains glisten sheenest,
  Where the lady-fern grows strongest,
  Where the morning dew lies longest,
  Where the blackcock sweetest sips it,
  Where the fairy latest trips it ;
  Hie to haunts right seldom seen—
  Lovely, lonesome, cool, and green,
  Over bank and over brae,
  Hie away! hie away!

SIR WALTER SCOTT.

IT has often surprised me to see how anxious many people are to visit foreign lands, and who are constantly talking of the wonderful scenery of these, who, nevertheless, have left unvisited districts and places quite as grand, and perhaps more beautiful, in their own native land—hills and valleys over which if the clouds of vapour frequently roll, the sunbeams also often alight and flood with glory the mountain gorges, especially when the orb is sinking far in the west, and when his shadows are lengthening on moor and fell, and his departing rays are being flashed back on lonely lochs, bald mountain peaks, mirrored in the ocean depths, a thousand fathoms down; and where the dark pine trees on the hill sides, or in the vales below, seem as if on fire when his last beams glow on tower and tree, on the glassy sea which quivers and quakes round our rock-bound coasts, and on the many islands which stud the bosom of the ocean away to the north-west of the mainland. With never any great desire to visit foreign lands, I had an early and an ardent desire to see both our own northern and southern Highlands. I had, indeed, a long and a great desire to be able one day to visit two distant lands, but not those generally trod by tourists—France, Italy, and Switzerland—but those of Egypt and Palestine, the latter especially. Now, however, I can only console myself with the thought that if I cannot see that ancient river, the Nile, which yielded us our earliest civilisation, I have at least seen the Ayr, the Tay, the Forth, and as Wordsworth says, " with the Tweed have travelled "—rivers far more known to song than the muddy Nile; and that though I may never see the old Jerusalem, " the lost capital of Jehovah," I can cherish " a good hope through grace " of one day seeing the " new Jerusalem which is above, where the over-topping palm trees grow, and where the still waters murmur from the eternal hills."

Fresh from reading and re-reading " Rob Roy," " The Fair Maid of Perth," and " The Lady of the Lake " of Sir Walter Scott, I, in 1848, set out for Perth and part of the Perthshire Highlands, my companion being a jolly New Cumnock farmer, the late Mr Wm. Arthur, then of Wellhill. Going by Edinburgh, we spent a day there, and then on Friday, August 4, visited Perth. Arriving there in the evening, we found that the Queen and Prince Albert were also passing through to the north, and that therefore all the gentry of the district and from great distances round had come into the town, and having occupied every inn and hotel, we could get no admission, or at least no bed in any of them. The private houses to which we had been directed being also filled, we found ourselves homeless strangers with no one able to take us in; but we took things coolly, and the night being dry, warm, and beautiful, we determined on going out to and spending it on the hill of Kinnoul, on the left bank of the Tay, a little way out of town, and were bending our steps thither when—then the dusk of the evening—we accidentally but most fortunately met a former schoolmaster of Old Cumnock—Mr M'Kinnell, then residing in Perth—who, learning our plight, at once took us to his house and entertained us in the kindest manner. The railway then did not extend beyond Perth, and so next day we went by coach to Dunkeld, which, with the surrounding country, charmed us exceedingly. In the afternoon we went on to Aberfeldy, and the day being Saturday we passed the Sabbath there, and like good Christians went to the morning service; but as the afternoon one was in Gaelic we went off to the hills, and with the aid of a powerful glass—the atmosphere being clear—we had an excellent view of the beautiful mountainous country and the valley of the Tay which lay stretched out before us. In the early morning of the following day we went out to view the Falls of Moness and "the birks of Aberfeldy," and thought of Robert Burns viewing the very same scenes where he conceived, if he did not then write his fine song, in which he thus refers to these picturesque falls :—

> " The braes ascend like lofty wa's,
> The foaming stream deep roaring fa's,
> O'erhung wi' fragrant spreading shaws,
>   The birks of Aberfeldy.

> " The hoary cliffs are crown'd wi' flowers,
> White o'er the linn the burnie pours,
> And rising, weets wi' misty showers
>   The birks of Aberfeldy."

Taking coach we drove away into the great range of savage hills surmounted by Ben Lawers looking down upon Loch Tay, a lovely sheet of water some 15 miles in length, at the western end of which is Killin, as pretty a spot as it is possible to conceive; from which, however, to the head of Loch Lomond the drive was through a country rugged but grand. In sailing down the loch we had a short but terrific thunderstorm, when from the bowels of the dense dark clouds which shrouded us in their grim chambers the lightning bolts darted out with fearful brightness, the thunder peals following almost instantaneously with fearful crash and roar, while the rain fell in such volume that in an instant the whole side of the lofty Ben Lomond was white with foaming torrents; and the storm passing off as suddenly as it came, and the sun shining out, the hill, with its gushing, leaping, smoking torrents, presented a sight never to be forgotten. Sailing to the foot of the loch, we ascended again to Inversnaid, where we landed, and were driven over the hill by a rough road in a jolting car to Loch Katrine, the sail on which, to its eastern end, in the little *Rob Roy* steamer, with the grand mountain gorge of the Trossachs, Ben Venue, and Ben Ann in front of us, with Ben Ledi in the distance, was charming. We climbed Ben Ann in the evening and passed the night at the Trossachs Inn, and next day, after exploring the Trossachs and the shores of Loch Achray, we returned again to Loch Lomond, and managed to get to the Isle of Bute in the evening, where we spent the next day viewing the old ruined castle with much interest, and thinking of the warlike Brandanes of old and of the bold and daring Norwegians who so often made war upon Bute in these old times. Next day we arrived at our home lying between the Lugar and the Nith, I at least, even after this short excursion, coming to the very easy conclusion that, after all, "there is no place like home."

Next year, anxious to see the poetic regions of the Tweed, the Ettrick, and the Yarrow, and in company with my youngest brother Thomas, and an excellent and intelligent Cumnock man, John Connell, both of whom still survive, and both men of poetic tastes, lively, and intelligent, we started in the second week of September 1849 for Edinburgh, going by the circuitous way of the Trossachs, Callender, and Stirling, sailing from the latter place down the Forth to Granton, where we arrived on a Saturday; and spending the Sabbath in Edinburgh, we went by coach next day to Peebles, all the country round blushing in its richest early autumnal beauty. Passing the evening there we went out early next morning and visited Neidpath Castle, a hoary old fortalice, now roofless, overlooking a beautiful bend of the Tweed, and after breakfast started with knapsack on back and staff in hand to walk on foot to Melrose, some twenty miles distant. The whole region is one of great beauty, and a land of song as well; and it was with strange feelings that

we paased Ashestiel, on the other side of the Tweed, and
gazed upon what in " Marmion " Scott calls—

> " The little steepy linn,
> That hems our little garden in."

It was here that Sir Walter's happiest days were spent,
before he aspired to found a Border family, and became
a Border laird.

When we reached Galashiels, and had gone into an inn
for a drink of ale, or some refreshment, we found the
town in great alarm, the cholera having broken out in it
that day. Pushing on we arrived at Melrose, and after
dinner viewed the town and its environs, and, of course,
the abbey, grand even in its ruins, and in the evening were
resting in the commercial room of the inn, which was then
pretty full of people, when a well dressed and comparatively
young man rushed into the room in a state of great excite-
ment, rang the bell, and cried out to the waiter to bring a
doctor at once, as he was in for cholera. After looking at
him for a moment or two, all those present rose and left
the room save myself and my two companions. Soon the
waiter returned saying that there was not a doctor to be
got, which made him more excited still. Looking at him,
I thought I would try my hand at prescribing for him, and
going up to him I asked him quietly, but firmly, to tell me
if he had not been drinking too freely ? He confessed that
he had, but had taken but little that day ; and I saw that
he was half in the " horrors," and telling the waiter to
take a pail of hot water to his bedroom (for, being a
commercial traveller, he had stayed there before), I accompanied him thither, and, bathing his feet, put him to bed,
after giving him nearly a gill of the best brandy made
into toddy, when—seeing that I did not desert him—he
grew calm ; and telling him to ring if he grew worse
and I would come to him and get a doctor brought to
him, I left him, and on visiting him in the morning I found
that he had slept well, and was better. I left him, he
uttering thanks and heaping blessings on my head ; and
I neither saw nor heard of him till, one night, four years
after, he came to me with extended arms at Kilmarnock

railway station. I did not at first know him, but he knew me, and warmly thanked me for standing by him at Melrose, when but for that he was certain that from drink and fear together, he would have died of the dreaded disease.

Early next morning we rose with the lark, and going up saw the sun rise from the top of the Eildon Hills. The view then of the country was surpassingly lovely, and also most extensive, taking in the distant Cheviot and Lammermuir Hills in different directions, with the braes of Yarrow, Teviotdale, the Merse, the classic Cowden Knowes, and Dryburgh, where rests the ashes of the great Sir Walter Scott—great as a poet, greater as a novelist, and great and good as a man. Driving down to Dryburgh, we stood uncovered before his tomb, giving it "the worship of silence." It is a beautiful spot, but I felt as it were oppressed by the great granite block of several tons weight which has been placed over his grave, and as I stood there and thought how that fertile brain was now still and at rest for ever, I remembered these fine lines of Charles Swain, the Manchester poet, on the burial of Sir Walter—

" The vision and the voice are o'er, their influence died away,
Like music o'er a summer lake at the golden close of day ;
The vision and the voice are o'er, but when shall be forgot,
The buried genius of romance, the imperishable Scott ! "

Returning, we drove to Abbotsford, "that romance in stone and mortar," as Washington Irving has so well named this shrine of the greatest genius to which Scotland ever gave birth ; and it was with the deepest interest, but with a feeling of inexpressible sadness, that I wandered through the apartments, gazed upon his books, and more especially on the last suit of clothes the mighty magician wore, and the staff upon which he last leaned ; and I was almost glad to get away from the place, beautiful and thrillingly interesting though it was ; and driving on to Selkirk, we had dinner in the Fleece Inn, in front of which is a statue of Sir Walter. From thence we sped on, and up the green, poetical Yarrow, past

H

Bowhill, and the old ruined castle of Newark; and I remembered that just eighteen years before our visit, or in the autumn of 1831, and just before Sir Walter left for Italy in the vain search for health, which it was found to be, he, the poet Wordsworth, and a few other choice friends —all now gone to the land of silence—had visited the spot, and stood in the shadow of that ruined castle grey; and this last visit to the place of both of them, and alas! too, the last meeting of the poets. Wordsworth, three years after, commemorated in his charming poem of " Yarrow Revisited," from which, because of its plaintive, though unsurpassed beauty, I will be excused for quoting these lines :—

> " Once more by Newark's castle-gate,
>   Long left without a warder,
> I stood, looked, listened, and with thee,
>   Great Minstrel of the Border.
>
> " Eternal blessings on the Muse,
>   And her divine employment ;
> The blameless Muse, who trains her sons
>   For hope and calm enjoyment ;
> Albeit sickness, lingering yet,
>   Has o'er their pillow brooded,
> And Care waylays their steps—a sprite
>   Not easily eluded.
>
> " For thee, O Scott! compelled to change
>   Green Eildon-hill and Cheviot
> For warm Vesuvius' vine-clad slopes,
>   And leave thy Tweed and Teviot.
> For mild Sorento's breezy waves,
>   May classic Fancy, linking
> With native Fancy, her fresh aid,
>   Preserve thy heart from sinking !
>
> " O ! while they minister to thee,
>   Each vying with the other,
> May Health return to mellow Age,
>   And Strength, her venturous brother ;
> And Tiber, and each brook and rill,
>   Renowned in song and story,
> With unimagined beauty shine,
>   Nor lose one ray of glory."

Strength did not return, but Scott returned, though only to die; but he has left that behind him which will never die, but which will continue to delight and instruct mankind as long as Time continues its march.   After visiting lone St Mary's Lake and the loch of The Lowes, we turned up the nearly as famous Ettrick stream, trudging it again on foot, passed Altrive Lake, the residence of that marvellous moorland genius, James Hogg, the Ettrick Shepherd, sat beside and pulled gowans from off his grave in Ettrick Churchyard, saw and stood in Boston's pulpit in the church; passed over the hill above the famous Bodsbeck, got on to the road a little way beyond it, and after a further walk of some six or seven miles arrived at Moffat, where we reposed our weary limbs for the night, and next day, taking coach to Dumfries, did homage at the grave of Burns, saw Thomas Aird (of whom I have previously spoken), and the day following (Saturday, 22nd September) took coach up the almost matchless valley of the Nith, and reached home in the breezy uplands of Cumnock, and

" Already tired of wandering o'er the world,
    Our homebound fancy ran her bark ashore."

CHAPTER XIII

PILGRIMAGES TO COVENANTING SHRINES

" Yes, though the sceptic's tongue deride
Those martyrs who for conscience died,
Though modish history blight their fame
And sneering courtiers hoot the name
Of men who dared alone be free
Amidst a nation's slavery,
Yet long for them the poet's lyre
Shall wake its notes of heavenly fire;
Their names shall nerve the patriot's hand
Upraised to save a sinking land,
And piety shall learn to burn
With holier transports o'er their urn."

THOMAS PRINGLE.

FROM a very early period of my life I had been taught to know something of the long struggle between the later Stuart Kings and the Scottish people, during the seventeenth century, for absolute and arbitrary rule in Church and State on the part of the Kings and on the part of the people for the maintenance of the Church as established by law, and especially for liberty of conscience and the right to worship God in their own way, holding to the Presbyterian form of worship, and refusing to become Episcopalians at the bidding of the King, at whose arbitrary and persecuting conduct I wondered much, and that men and women should have been banished and sold for slaves to Barbadoes by the hundred, and not only so, but put to death on the scaffold and shot down like wild beasts of the field, and all because they would not worship God as the King commanded, and because they held by the Kirk which had been established by law. For this really was the sole reason why the people then were so treated; for had they quietly consented to do as they were bid, even in matters spiritual, there would have been no persecution, no banishing, hangings, shootings in the fields, and drownings in the estuaries of the sea. Because, therefore, the people maintained the right not only to worship God as conscience pointed out the way, but entered into a solemn covenant with God and with one another to do so, and to maintain the Presbyterian form of worship and Church government, they were subjected to long years of fiery persecution and death.

> " And all to please a worthless thing
>   As ere disgraced the name of King."

But firm and unyielding they stood, until even passive cowardice was warmed, and the pig-headed King James VII. became so oppressed with fear and dread that the priest-ridden poltroon tyrant fled from the land which he had not only misgoverned but deluged with blood, and in the end leaving fawning courtiers and his friends to gaze upon a dissolved Court and a vacant throne!

It was the pious, enthusiastic, and patriotic James Renwick—the last martyr of the Covenant—who once said that " the mountains and moors of Scotland were flowered with martyrs' graves." These graves in the south and west of Scotland my father had long known, and very early in life he took me to several of them. That of the five martyrs on the Loan, at Mauchline, was the first I had gazed upon, and that to the boy-martyr of Sorn, George Wood, the second. The Mauchline martyrs, who were all hanged there in 1686 without trial, were not natives of the place; but the Sorn martyr belonged to the parish, and at the age of only sixteen was shot by a savage trooper named John Reid, fully a mile east of the village, and it was with peculiar awe and loathing at the brutal deeds that I listened to the tragic tales and gazed upon their tombs. Richard Cameron fascinated my youthful mind as much as did " Wallace wight, or Bruce the bold ; " and so long ago as the summer of 1832, on a week-day, I was taken with my father and mother to what is familiarly known as " Cameron's Stone," in the lone and wild Ayrs Moss, to hear the late Rev. Dr William Symington, then of Stranraer, afterwards of Glasgow, preach a sermon, and hold other religious services on that historic battlefield. Although he was a great orator—famed even in the city of Glasgow—yet, being but young, I remember but little of the service save the first Psalm that was sung, the 74th, beginning with the mournful plaint—

> " O God, why hast thou cast us off?
>   Is it for evermore?
>   Against Thy pasture sheep why doth
>   Thine anger smoke so sore?"

I was greatly awed when the breeze-borne notes were wafted far over the moor, startling the wild fowl of the bleak wilderness, and the shepherds watching their flocks; and I was much alarmed when at the close of the services a man fainted or fell down in a fit and lay there stretched out on the moor with the people about him trying to restore him, which by and by they succeeded in doing.   There was no tall obelisk set up at the grave of the hero-preacher then, but only a broad stone with a long inscription thereon, on which also were carved a drawn sword and an open Bible, as related by James Hyslop—then only five years dead—in that noble burst of piety and patriotism—" The Cameronian Dream "—

> " Where Cameron's sword and his Bible are seen
>   Engraved on the stone where the heather grows green."

Two years later I went with my father to hear the late Rev. John Carslaw, of Airdrie, preach at " lone Lochgoin," far up in the wilds of Fenwick, and so much progress had I made in learning in these two brief years, that I was able to take down the whole heads and particulars of his great and eloquent discourse.   Previous to this I had also visited the monument raised to the brave Captain Paton of Meadowhead, in Fenwick churchyard.   In 1835 I walked from within two miles of Fenwick to Bothwell Bridge, and back the same day to hear the same great preacher—the Rev. John Carslaw—discourse to a congregation of from ten to twelve thousand rapt and most attentive listeners, and I well remember that, in closing his discourse, he said that parting was always a matter of great seriousness with him, and so with lofty and burning eloquence he pressed home his Gospel message, his eye kindling, and his lip quivering with emotion. I can see the scene perfectly yet with my mind's eye. The westering sun shone brightly, the light breeze of the former part of the day had died away, and hardly a leaf quivered on these fair and lovely Bothwell banks, and as the preacher gave out the last Psalm the soft and gentle murmur of the Clyde was heard, as its waters, which had ever and unceasingly glided by since on that disastrous day, 21st June, 1679, the stream ran red with the blood of the divided and greatly outnumbered Covenanters, went babbling by on their way to join the all-devouring sea, and as they mingled their own peculiar tune with the music of Mr Carslaw's voice, as in earnest, pleading words he offered up the closing prayer, and helped to swell the "grave sweet melody" of the parting song of praise, which, on the wings of faith and true devotion swelled and rose beyond the empyrean. No one who heard it and was present to hear and to witness the whole scene can ever have forgotten it.

Many times also now, and from a very early period of my life, I have stood upon the battlefield of Drumclog—

"Where Loudounhill looks o'er his bog
    Still smiling proudly on Drumclog;
    Where Claverse, in his mad career
    Of ruthless murder learn'd to fear
    A bold though simple peasantry,
    Who stood for God and liberty";

and many an earnest and eloquent discourse during all these passing years have I heard upon that stirring historic field.

Priesthill, too, I have often visited on week-day and on Sabbath, and stood on the site of the ruined cot of "The Christian carrier," and pictured to myself the dark, tragic, and bloody deed of that May morning, when in that lonely wilderness, the bloody Graham of Claverhouse caused the meek and quiet John Brown—who had

been at no armed rising or rebellion against the tyrannical
rulers of " that iron time "—to be shot at his own door in
presence of his wife with a babe in her arms and a little
child at her side, and another about to be born, the
murderer riding off with a scoffing taunt upon his lips ;
and I could fancy the agonized, weeping, and new-made
widow with her affrighted little ones alone with her in
that terrible hour, while the heartless slayer of God's
dear saint and his cavalcade rode away across the wild,
their armour ringing through the misty morning air,
scaring the hill-birds as they rode away from blood to
blood, petrifying with fear the dwellers in those desolate
wilds where few people dwelt.

After coming to the Cumnock district, I took frequent
walks alone to the Martyrs' Monument on Crossgellioch
hill, about three miles south of the town of Old Cumnock,
where in the days of " darkness and blood," three men
were shot down in cold blood, in July 1685, when coming from hearing the youthful James Renwick preach in
the neighbourhood of Dalmellington.   Once when wandering alone on this hill, writing one of my earliest poems,
the subject of it being " The Martyrdom " enacted there,
I was caught in one of those thunderstorms which often
gather and burst among the hills.   Lingering and musing
there one summer afternoon, more than half a century ago,
I wist not of a gathering blackness away down in the west,
and engrossed in thought I heeded not the deep gloom that
was brooding over me until I was startled by a vivid flash
of lightning, and the almost instantaneous crash of a
terrific peal of thunder which " shook the vaulted sky " ;
when almost at once the *eerie* silence which had reigned
around was broken by the loud rushing of the tempest of
wind which came careering over the moor ; for a whirl-
wind swept along the wild, and raved round the Martyrs'
lonely sepulchre.   The lightning ran along the face of
the dense dark thundercloud, or darted out in forked
tongues of lurid flame ; while ever and anon the deep
dread voice of the thunder bellowed long and loud making
the wide and lonesome wilderness to quake.   The rain
rushed in torrents from the dark and frowning heavens,

and mingled with heavy hailstones rattled on the face of the affrighted earth! I was appalled by the violence of the storm, and cowered close to the Martyrs' Monument for shelter, but in less than half an hour it had expended its fury, its dregs passing away to the east, and all at once the cheering sun again shone out and his bright and gladsome beams soon restored me to my former calmness of spirit.

In after years I visited the Martyrs' Stone at Cairn, overlooking the windings of the Nith, between New Cumnock and Kirkconnel, where two Covenanters—named Hair and Corson, were shot on the same day as those of Crossgellioch, and by the same persons—Colonel James Douglas and a party of dragoons. I had also stood at the old Market Cross of Sanquhar, where the heroic Richard Cameron, and twenty others, published the famous Declaration in the summer 1680, in which they disowned the authority of the profligate, cruel and per-jured Charles II., " as forfeited by his perjury and breach of covenant both to God and to His kirk, and usurpation of His crown and royal prerogatives therein, and many other breaches in matters ecclesiastical, and by his tyranny and breaches of the very *leges regnandi* in matters civil." I have also gone up the lonely Enterkine Pass, where the Covenanters obtained a signal victory over the Royal troops, and rescued several prisoners, who were being carried to prison and death, and have stood beside the grave of the holy Daniel M'Michael, who was barbarously shot in the beautiful, though hardly less lonely, Dalveen Pass, among the lofty Lowther hills in the centre of Dumfriesshire; and I have lingered in St Michael's Churchyard, Dumfries, in which several martyrs of the Covenant lie in their bloody graves. I have also stood within the ivy-covered walls of Samuel Rutherford's church at Anwoth, by the side of which is the grave of John Bell of Whiteside, who with several others were shot at the instance of the bloody laird of Lagg on Kirkconnel Hill in the parish of Tongueland. I have stood uncovered at the grave of the aged widow and the virgin martyr who were drowned by cruel and unfeeling men, tied to stakes in Blednoch Bay, where they sang praises to God while the tide rose higher and higher until the foaming billows of the salt sea brine went boiling over their heads. I have stood with awe in the Greyfriars churchyard, Edinburgh, the scene of shocking barbarities for months after the disastrous battle of Bothwell Bridge; and I have visited Glen Trool, at the head of the river Cree, where in its amphitheatre of hills some of the sons of the Covenant were slain in "the killing time"; I have visited many other Covenanting scenes far in wilds unknown to public view. I was also mainly instrumental in getting a beautiful and enduring granite monument erected at Cumnock to the memory of "Peden the prophet"; and another at Lochgoin to the plodding, pious John Howie, the excellent biographer of so many of the Covenanters; and what I said of the former monument at its inauguration by Professor Blackie some fourteen years ago, applies equally to the other, and also to the martyrs of the Covenant—"The lapse of centuries and the corroding tooth of Time may cause even that granite pile to crumble into dust. But even though such should be the case, still the memory of such men as Peden, and of the pious and heroic Covenanters can never perish, for they are star-traced in the heavens." The more I consider that grand and ultimately triumphant struggle for liberty, civil and religious, the more I feel inclined to say with a true though anonymous poet—

> " The hero's palm, the martyr's crown,
>   The patriot's deathless name,
> From age to age shall hand thee down
>   First in the ranks of fame.
> Our fathers loved thy rugged strand,
>   They sleep beneath thy sod;
> And mine shall be my father's land,
>   And mine my father's God."

CHAPTER XIV

SOME MEN AND AUTHORS I HAVE KNOWN

" Man is the nobler growth our realms supply,
And souls are ripened in our northern sky."
                                        Mrs Barbauld.

" Greatness and goodness are not means, but ends!
Hath he not always treasures, always friends,
The good, great man?   Three treasures, love and light
And calm thoughts, regular as infants' breath;
And three firm friends, more sure than day and night,
Himself, his Maker, and the angel Death."
                                        S. T. Coleridge.

ALL my life I have been much more anxious to converse with authors through their books than to make their personal acquaintance and to talk with them face to face. Too often when I have done the latter I have been sadly disappointed, and instead of finding that their feet only were partly clay, like the great image which the King of Babylon saw in his dream, they were altogether clay, without the head of gold—and rather inferior clay too. This was mostly, however, the case with the fourth-rate and obscure aspirants for poetical fame. It was, I found, wonderful what really good individual poems many of these authors would write; though, when I came to converse with them, I found them to be the most ignorant, conceited fools imaginable—thirsting and fishing for praise in the most barefaced and disgusting fashion. Some few I found professing to be more lax in morals than I believe they really were, and wishing to be thought like Byron in this respect. Others thought it manly to get drunk, and thus to " glory in their shame," because Burns was thought too often to " err in vision and stumble in judgment," through strong drink. The vanity, too, of many of these creatures was inordinate; and I was surprised to find that this was far less the case, and always in a far less degree, with the lady authors than with the male sex, which, from what I have seen and known of them otherwise, was always a very great surprise to me. I have found, too, that the loftier the genius, the greater the ability, and the more an author was famed, the more humble and unassuming that author was.

One of the earliest of my literary acquaintances and friends was the poetical editor of Dumfries—Thomas Aird —a truly great and good man, and the author of several volumes of both prose and poetry of great power, exalted genius, and exquisite finish. But of him I have already spoken.

I never chanced to either see or hear the late Rev. Dr Guthrie, though I have read some of his books—" The Gospel in Ezekiel," and " The City : its Sins and Sorrows " —but I once had a long and a most pleasant letter of thanks from him. He had been lecturing in London, and there and in other places he quoted " The Land o' Leal " as one of the songs of Burns. I could not help feeling sorry that a man so much admired, so great, good, and so worthy of all the fame he had gained, should go on repeating the blunder, which I felt sure some one would discover and make public, and so I took it upon me to write him and to point out that the song was not written by Burns, but by the Baroness Nairne, and told him where he would find the proofs of it, and had a long letter of thanks for doing so.

Miss Aird, of Kilmarnock, I got acquainted with soon after the publication of her first volume—" The Home of the Heart "—in 1846. Although some of the pieces in that volume are a little slim, one poem—" The E'enin' Fa' " is one of the finest poems in our native Doric ; anything it wants in power it more than makes up for by its beauty, tenderness and its pathos. An excellent Christian woman, she became rather hypochondriacal in her latter years.

Of Sarah Parker, " The Irish Girl," I also knew something. She was the least poetical person in appearance I ever looked upon ; and yet she had gifts in that way of no mean order. The title of her first volume—" The

Opening of the Sixth Seal," was unfortunate, while really it opened nothing !

Hugh Brown, a native of Newmilns and for years schoolmaster in Galston, was a poet of a higher order than either of the two ladies just noticed; his lengthy poem, " The Covenanters," being lofty and grand, and written in ringing, harmonious verse. When age and indigence overtook him, I was delighted at being able, from the representations I made to the late Mr W. E. Gladstone, and the specimens of his poetry I forwarded to him, to get that noble-minded man to send him a gift of £50 from the Royal Bounty Fund.

John G. Ingram, painter and poet, another Ayrshire man with a most erratic nature, was possessed of more original genius and greater power than Mr Brown; but being unfortunate in his marriage his nature became soured and somewhat misanthropic in his latter years; but his poem " The Angel of Hope," one of considerable length, has all the richness and gushing beauty of Moore, while his " Dream of Another World " is a powerful Byronic-like production. In 1875, when the sere leaves were falling from the trees, he " went his eternal way " at the age of threescore and ten.

Good, kindly, social, old Archibald M'Kay, of Kilmarnock, was a genius of a different stamp. He possessed a large amount of true, pawky Scots humour, with the skill to construct a tale or lilt a song. He was also an excellent prose writer, and his " History of Kilmarnock " will ever remain a monument of his skill and industry.

Of all the lady poets I have ever known, the late Mrs Harriet Stuart Menteath—sister-in-law of the late Lady Menteath of Mansefield, New Cumnock—was cut and away far above and beyond any other. Her " Lays of the Kirk and Covenant," first published in 1851, have gone through several editions. Mrs Menteath was not only the poet of the greatly wronged, and still frequently maligned Covenanters, but she was also the sweet and cultured poet and interpreter of Nature. Her poem on " The Martyrs of Wigtown," with its murmur loud and cadence low is a production of moving, thrilling power, and of charming execution. In the lengthened correspondence I had with her while, with her husband, she resided in the Basses Pyrenees, her letters of great beauty and grace showed how exalted was her nature and how truly Christian was her character. She died some fourteen years ago, after having sent me some of her unpublished poems.

With the late Mr William M'Dowall, of Dumfries, editor, historian, and poet, I was also well acquainted. His "Nithsdale Martyrs" is among the best poems which have been written on the Covenanting struggle. A weird-looking man, he was at the same time one of the best men I have ever known. Nearly twenty years have now passed by since at the age of seventy-four he was laid to rest beneath the Ash tree in Troqueer Churchyard, of which he himself had sung in exalted strains.

I have had two visits from Mr Wallace Bruce, the poet, while Consul at Edinburgh for the United States of America. He is a pleasing poet, an eloquent lecturer, and a most agreeable gentleman.

With that extraordinary man, Dr Andrew Carnegie, I have met on three occasions; twice in Cumnock, and once in Ayr. The first time he was driving from the South of England to the North of Scotland, and was accompanied by his venerable mother, to whom he was devotedly and beautifully attached. The second time he was accompanied by his charming wife and winning little daughter. On this occasion he did me the honour of sending me an invitation to meet him at the hotel, which I did, and was delighted by his strong, good sense, and the extent of his information on literary men and matters. His own cultured style, and also the far-reaching political wisdom which shine out in his works surprise me more than his great wealth; especially in one whose life has been so long and so largely devoted to business. He has done me the honour of sending me numbers of his published works, which I value very highly.

With the late Dr Charles Rogers, of the Grampian Club and Wallace Monument notoriety, I was intimate. He was a man of excellent talents and great force of character. It has, however, been rightly said that he was a book maker, but not an author, and he will be longest remembered for his connection with the Stirling Wallace Monument, and with very many other monuments to the notable dead all over the country, and these lines of the late witty Lord Neaves, on a projected monument to that eccentric old judge, Lord Monboddo, who traced the origin of man back to and sprung from the monkey long before Charles Darwin's day, will also keep him in remembrance—

> " Let Noel Paton make the plan,
>   And Rogers give the nod O—
> A monkey rising to a man,
>   In honour of Monboddo ! "

I was for a time associated with him in one monumental undertaking, and I was sorry when we had to part company, and more sorry still when he altogether perverted and altered the information I gave him about Burns' "Holy Willie" and other matters, and succeeded in changing the beliefs of the late learned and excellent Dr Edgar of Mauchline on these matters, and in—for a little while—causing a rupture between myself and that excellent man also. Dr Rogers, perhaps, had no real intention of doing what resulted from his dubious course of action, and as to him I owed not a little in several respects, I think kindly of him still.

The Old Benston schoolmaster, John Johnston, one of Lord Nelson's Trafalgar veterans—a gentleman by birth and education, though coming to great straits in his latter years—was one of the most intelligent men I ever knew; a poet, too, for in capital heroic verse he sang " The Battle of the Nile," and " The Battle of Trafalgar "; and never was the death of Nelson—the greatest of sea captains —sung so well as Mr Johnston did in these few lines :—

> " In torrid climes, where Nature pants for breath
>   And tainted gales bring pestilence and death,
> Nelson had sought, but long had sought in vain,
>   The still retreating fleets of France and Spain ;
> When found at last, he crushed them on the flood,
>   And sealed the awful conquest with his blood."

Grand lines surely for an old schoolmaster to write.   After having served twelve years in the Navy he obtained his discharge, but without a pension, and after teaching a wayside school for many years with the burden of ninety years pressing him down, he was forced to apply to the parish for relief, when he was granted the paltry sum for himself and daughter of 3s. 6d. a week.   I thought it right then, when the old man was placed in such painful circumstances, to make an appeal for him to the public; and in a letter which I published in the leading newspapers of the kingdom, I among other things said: "What a pity, nay what a disgrace, it is that one who perilled his life for his country in the most eventful crisis in her history, should be forced to join the poor and eat the parish bread; and the utterly insufficient sum of 3s. 6d. a week is all his country has to bestow on one who took part in the great and glorious achievements performed by the brave defenders of our much-loved sea-girt isle! The blood of multitudes of these brave men who battled so long for their country has tinged the ocean waves in almost every clime, while their bones repose far down in the deep sea caves, or whiten the hills of almost every country under heaven; and while, in the eloquent language of General Sir William Napier, 'their merits are forgotten, and the few survivors wander for the most part indigent and neglected, or insulted by the wealth protected by the valour of the now despised veteran.'"   To the honour of humanity, I in a few weeks received gifts of fully £65 for the old man.   The first arrived and was handed to him when all he and his dutiful daughter had with them in the house was one small three-halfpenny loaf of bread and one halfpenny in money!   I also applied on his behalf to the Admiralty, and in less than a month (Mr Gladstone's Government was then in power) I received notice that the old veteran had been granted a pension of £27, 7s. yearly, and which, thankful and happy, he enjoyed for nine years, dying on 1st September, 1880, aged ninety-nine years and forty-one days.   Of having been able thus successfully to befriend these two aged men—Hugh Brown, as already stated, and the old Trafalgar veteran in a much greater degree, I felt and still feel more proud than I ever was of any achievement of my life.

As secretary of the Peden and Lochgoin Covenanters' monuments, I had some curious experiences and insight into the nature and disposition of not a few men. Knowing that the first Marquis of Argyll had been beheaded for his strong Covenanting principles in 1661, the year after he had been instrumental in bringing back the perfidious Charles II. from exile and setting the crown upon his worthless head, I was induced to send the Duke of Argyll one of the sheets containing the appeal for funds to raise a monument over the grave of old "Peden, the Prophet," at Cumnock, when, although his Grace did not comply with the request, he was courteous enough to reply, and which he did in the following terms :—

"Sir,—I am very sorry that the claims upon me by the living are so urgent that I have been obliged to decline subscribing to memorials for the dead.—Yours obediently,

"ARGYLL."

This letter fully convinced me that the noble Duke—the great MacChaillan More—did his alms in the manner laid down by Christ—"When thou doest thine alms, let not thy left hand know what thy right hand doeth." And that the Duke acted strictly upon this scriptural principle is clear from the fact that no one—so far as I have ever been able to learn—ever heard of any of his acts of generosity to the living. If, however, all men had acted in the matter of memorials to the dead, as the Duke did, though out of care and kindness for the living, of course, and as he so plainly told me, then the costly monument recently erected to his great ancestor, the first Marquis of Argyle—a good Christian, though a rather slippery statesman, and the most pusillanimous General of an army—would never have been raised.

The Duke, however, did not stand alone in giving the cold shoulder to the Peden memorial movement; for to a like application the Provost of a certain Royal Burgh in the south, noted for its Covenanting memories, made no reply whatever; while the rather heavy and dull historian of that same burgh, and who had written largely and

I

eulogistically on the Covenanters—worse still than the Duke of Argyle—wrote that he declined to aid the monument because "in a little while the living would not have room to walk the earth for memorials set up to the dead!" I do not exactly know whether it was the dread of this, or because he, a servant, aspired to rule his masters, which soon after caused him to go to America where, of course, he would find more room and fewer monuments.

One of the most strange and weird-looking men of note I have ever met with was the late Mark Napier, author of " The Life and Times of Montrose," " Memorials of Graham of Claverhouse," and other works. He was a Jacobite of the Jacobites long after these supporters and partisans of the " Pretender "—Charles Edward Stuart— had become extinct as a party. Having occasion to call upon him once in Edinburgh, shortly after the publication of his " Memorials of Claverhouse " was published, I was greatly impressed by his appearance. His face was rather long, thin, and very pale. His hair was long, and also his beard, and both were white as the driven snow; and with the peculiar peering gleam of his clear, blue eye, which reminded me of that—as described by Coleridge—of *The Ancient Mariner*; or rather, as a whole, I thought of the portraits I had seen of that old slayer of the Covenanters— General Dalziel of Binns. In appearance and manners he was altogether " a gentleman of the old school "—stately but most courteous. After some little conversation on general topics, it drifted on to literature, when he remarked, with a smile, that " a good deal of his time had been taken up with defending bad characters." I think I see yet the peculiar twinkle of his blue eye and slight smile when I replied " I was glad to hear him confess that they were bad characters." His manner then, and the proofs which he must have known, convinced me then, and convince me still, that Mr Napier did not himself believe in his contradiction of the reported drowning of the two women at Wigtown in that terrible year of persecution— 1685—but that he meant it to be, what it really was, a piece of special pleading, which, however, was utterly demolished by the masterly reply—" History Vindicated in the case of the Wigtown Martyrs "—by the late Rev. Alex. Stewart, D.D., minister of Glasserton.

With the late Professor Blackie I became acquainted fully sixteen years ago, doing so altogether quite by accident. He and Mrs Blackie had been making a tour in the west, and were staying one night at the Dumfries Arms Hotel, Cumnock, when, chancing to go into the commercial-room there, with two gentlemen on business, we found Professor Blackie alone, walking up and down in it. My friends and I were sitting, at the gloaming hour, in the recess of the oriel window, which looks out into the garden, when, occasionally pausing as he passed near to where we were, he looked out into the garden also, and at length made some remark which led to his taking a seat beside us. He said that when on a tour he always liked best to frequent the commercial or general business room, as he thus got acquainted with the people, which he could not do when keeping to his own private apartments. He soon told us that he had been up that afternoon at the old churchyard on Barrhill, and that standing beneath the old, hallowed twin thorns which distil the dews of the summer night upon the weird but saintly old Covenanter's grave, he had written a sonnet on the old prophet. Suddenly turning to me, whom, of course, he did not know, he asked me if I knew anything about Peden, when I replied that I knew, I thought, nearly all that could now be known concerning him. Had I written anything about him? he asked. I replied that I had, when he expressed a great desire to see it, and next morning I handed him a copy of what I had published a short time before in an Edinburgh magazine, and which now forms Chapter IV., of the first series of my "Homes, Haunts, and Battlefields of the Covenanters." After his return home he wrote me expressing his thanks for the pleasure and the information which the perusal of the article had given him. In the conversation I had with him in Cumnock, he had spoken of the propriety of having a monument worthy of the grand old praying Covenanter erected to his memory at Cumnock, and he stated that if a movement for that purpose was set on foot he would gladly become a member of the committee, and would also give a donation towards the cost of it.   This was done, and well the grand old Professor kept his word, for besides contributing liberally towards the cost of it himself, he obtained several handsome sums for it from his friends. And not only this, but he aided the cause still further, for he came through and gave a lecture in the Town Hall, which was filled to overflowing and after paying expenses it yielded a sum of nearly £30 to the fund.   The monument—beautiful in design, and of enduring Aberdeen granite—was erected at the close of 1891, and in presence of a large gathering of between 3000 and 4000 persons was inaugurated by Professor Blackie on Thursday, 16th July, 1892.   In coming forward to do so, amid ringing applause, he said that "that moment was one of the proudest of his life.   Even if he had been made a D.D., LL.D., or a D.C.L. by all the Universities in Europe he would not have been so proud as he was of that day, that gathering, and that monument."   And he went on to make a noble defence of the Covenanters, whose first rising against the Government, at Pentland, he said was noble in sentiment, though unwise in policy.   "What made the Scots determined was that they would not sell their consciences for the King's favour.   Hence it was that, more than to Bannockburn, Scotland owed her character and love of freedom of conscience to the Covenanters.   Bruce at Bannockburn fought for political independence; the Covenanters fought for liberty of conscience.   Bruce did the business in a single battle; but the Covenanters had to fight for fifty years, and were butchered in the most abominable way.   Their butchers were a disgrace to humanity, and were worse than devils. Peden, that dear man of God, it was true, died in his bed, but that was only by a happy accident."   It is needless to say that such sentiments as these were warmly applauded by the man of Kyle.

That night the Professor was my guest, and in the beautiful summer evening we drove down through the grounds of Dumfries House, he stopping in front of the mansion, inspecting and reading a Greek inscription on a bust there with not a little curiosity.

At night we sat late talking of many things, but mostly of books and their authors; nor could he be persuaded to go earlier to bed, notwithstanding the fatiguing day he had had and that he was now past the far fourscore years. And when at length he did consent to go to his bedroom, and Mrs Todd told him to ring if anything went wrong with him, he said, briskly, "What will go wrong with me? I never lost half-an-hour's sleep with indigestion in my life!"

Next day we drove to the grave of brave and sturdy Richard Cameron in the "lone and wild Airsmoss," and as we crossed on foot the moor of nearly a mile in width, which lay between the highway and the monument, and which he did with the agility of a man of twenty-five, he told me the now well-known story of his respect for the picturesque plaid which he gene ally wore round his shoulders. When he received his first Professorship, he said, he was bare of money, yet Mrs Blackie (his noble wife of whom he ever spoke so warmly) would have him get a new black coat. This, he said, he could then ill afford, but got her to wrap her pretty plaid round his shoulders, which hid the bareness of the coat he had, giving him, at the same time, a picturesque appearance, and which he wore, and which he said "made him decent till money came in."

When we reached the monument on the eastern edge of the great morass he uncovered his head, and going round it he read the inscription and I described to him the now nearly effaced figures of a hand holding a sword, and an open Bible, across which could once be read— "The Word of God." Vaulting up on to the breast-high basement of the monument he asked the names of and I described to him the localities within view; and still uncovered and with his face turned towards the lofty Cairntable, he asked me if I could repeat James Hyslop's poem, "The Cameronian Dream," and to do so if I could. This I was able to do, the grand old man standing with closed eyes and face raised upwards, as if in rapt, calm, and deep devotion. "A grand poem, a noble flight of piety and patriotism," he exclaimed at the close. What a picture that would have been, I have often thought; we two alone there with the dead, standing on the basement of the monument, the Professor's long white locks waving in the light wind which wandered over that lonely wilderness, with the brightest of July suns shining down upon us.

Leaving the memorable spot, we recrossed the moor, regained our machine, and by invitation drove on through the town of Muirkirk to take lunch at the house of Glenbuck with Mr Charles Howatson, the genial laird "of that ilk," and others in the district. After dinner, at the request of Mrs Howatson, he sang his inimitable song of "Mrs Jenny Geddes" to the tune of "British Grenadiers," and when he came to this stanza, and flung the stool, the delight of the company was great and the laughter and applause loud—

"A bump! a thump! a smash! a crash! now gentle folks beware!
  Stool after stool, like rattling hail, came turling through the air,
  With, Well done, Jenny! bravo, Jenny! that's the proper tool!
  When the deil will oot and show his snout, just meet him with a stool!
  With a row-dow—at them now! there's naething like a stool!"

And with her three-legged stool Jenny thus stopped the "saying of Mass," as she supposed, in St Giles, and put the Dean, Council, and Bailies all to flight.

I had previously asked Professor Blackie if it was true, as reported, that he had sung "Scots wha hae" to the Sultan at Constantinople. "No," he replied, "but I have sung it on the top of Ben Nevis and on the top of the great Pyramid of Egypt. Accompanying him to Inches station, at the wild opening among the hills leading into Douglasdale, where he took the train for Edinburgh, I grasped his hand for the last time, waved him an adieu, and never saw him again! The last letter I received from him was written little more than three months before his death. It was dated 22nd November 1894, and in it he thus mournfully writes :—

"MY DEAR SIR,—I was delighted to see your well known hand again after so long a blank. 'Tis only too true, I am not the man I was. Some months ago I knew for the first time what old age meant, and am now suffering from asthma—a disease with little or no pain; brings weakness and weariness with it, from which I fear at my time of life—85 years—there is no hope of recovery. I immediately ordered two copies of your 'Songs of the Covenant.' Scotland has been only too apt to forget what she owes to these noble patriots. Your selection from my contribution is excellent; 'Renwick' is the most classical, as 'Jenny Geddes,' I hope, may one day, be the most popular. I wrote one also at Sanquhar on Cameron's dethronement of Charles II., which I am sorry does not appear in my published volume.

"Ever yours sincerely,
"J. S. BLACKIE."

Peace to his *manes*. He was the most plain, honest, out-spoken, kindly Christian man, I almost ever knew. Though not able to attend his funeral, I have since visited and dropped a sympathetic tear upon his grave in the Dean Cemetery, Edinburgh, in which he now takes his last, long, unbroken sleep.

One of the most cultured of our poets, a true son of genius, richly endowed of the Muses, and the most genial of men, was Mr William Freeland, so long the able editor of *The Glasgow Evening Times.* His volume, entitled " A Birth of Song and Other Poems," must long keep his memory green. It is a triumph of refined taste and genius.

Of equal culture and high achievement in the realms of poesy is the volume of the Rev. Thomas Dunlop, a Scotsman, though now south of the Tweed, somewhere on the banks of the Mersey. His muse has a fine ring, ever musical, instructive, and true. He, too, is as amiable as a man as he is gifted as a poet. His charming volume—

" John Tamson's Bairns and Other Poems," contains the best and most pleasing proofs of both.

With the late Rev. James Murray, author of "Songs of the Covenant Times" (1861) and several works in prose, I was on terms of close intimacy during nearly the whole course of his ministry at Cumnock. While the "Songs" are spirited and full of poetic fire, the lengthy historical introduction to the volume is most valuable. Mr Murray, in his work on Elisha the prophet, is not by any means dwarfed by the work on the same theme by the great German divine, Friedrich Adolf Krummacher. His brother, Robert E. Murray, minister of the neighbouring parish of New Cumnock, with whom I was on more intimate terms still, was also a poet of fair performance, and in 1871 published " The Dayspring from on High," which is both classical and pious. In 1881 he published "Notœ variorum: Physical and Metaphysical," a curious and interesting prose work, somewhat after the manner of White's "Natural History of Selborne," Both were learned and excellent men and ministers, and now I have to mourn them both in their graves.

" Alas for love if thou wert all
    And nought beyond, O earth ! "

Among what may be called the poets of labour with whom I have become more or less intimate, are Alexander Anderson, " Surfaceman " (a name, now, both he and others should drop); Wm. Aitken, a Catrine bard; James S. M'Culloch, of Carsphairn; H. C. Wilson, by birth a Cumnock man, now in England; and George G. B. Sproat, a well-to-do Galloway farmer—all men of sound sense, refined taste, and true poets, as their published volumes unmistakably show. The first two—Messrs Anderson and Aitken — have succeeded (Wordsworth's anathematizing of it notwithstanding) in making even the *railway* poetic, while they both sing naturally and well on many themes. Messrs Wilson and M'Culloch are also both sweet singers, more lyrical than the other two, the last-named having also an evident turn for narrative poetry. Mr Sproat is a master of pathos, and an excellent descriptive poet, while his volume—" The Rose of Dalma Linn and Other Lays of Gallowa' "—containing one of the finest poems on Robert Burns ever written.

With painters of note I have never been much acquainted. The only two of recognised excellence have both been Kilmarnock men—Mr A. S. Mackay, a portrait painter; and Mr John Curdie, of landscape fame. With the first (who but recently went the way of all the earth) I became acquainted more than fifty years ago, and not only was he one of the best portrait painters of his time, but he had an excellent taste for, and a large acquaintance with, polite literature. He was gentle in his manners, and kindly of heart above most men I have known. He painted the portraits of my venerable father and mother, and of myself, when I had more hair on my head than I have now; and he has left few behind him who mourn his death as deeply as I do.

Years and years have also come and gone since I first knew Mr Curdie (now also no more). He—so far as I know—painted only landscapes, and I have seen none better. Give him but a river scene with trees, and he could produce a picture which could fascinate and hold you like the "glittering eye" of "The Ancient Mariner" of Coleridge. Had either of these two artists only had the good fortune to have come in contact with and been employed to paint a portrait or a landscape for some Duke Marquis, or Earl, and thus got introduced into that "charmed circle," their fame as painters would have been world wide, and they would have left lasting names and fame behind them. But painters, like poets, too often experience the truth of what the poet of "The Minstrel" James Beattie—says and shows when he sings—

"How hard it is to climb
The steep where Fame's proud temple shines afar."

Besides those (among the poets) there were a great many others; some fairly gifted, some bad and some worse, of whom I will not speak. It is such troops of poetasters—for the most part vain, conceited fools—who cause so many of the strong-minded, hard-headed men of the world and of business so often to look upon the whole race of poets as *daft* and ready for Bedlam, whereas the true poet is the truest teacher—the prophet as well as the teacher; and for myself, the acquaintance with poetry which I have long had has, in the language of the elder Coleridge, "been to me its own exceeding great reward."

CHAPTER XV

AUTHORSHIP AND INCIDENTS

" Up! up! my Friend, and quit your books,
  Or surely you'll grow double:
Up! up! my Friend and clear your looks;
  Why all this toil and trouble?"
                                    —WILLIAM WORDSWORTH.

" Were others angry, I excused them too;
  Well might they rage, I gave them but their due."
                                    —ALEXANDER POPE.

FROM a very early period of my boyhood, books were my delight, and my solace in every time of youthful trouble, even although the books I had access to, when a boy, were not the best suited—one might think—for the young mind. The " Scots Worthies," of excellent, plodding, pious John Howie of Lochgoin; Crookshank's " History of the State and Sufferings of the Church of Scotland from the Restoration to the Revolution," with Brown's and Fisher's Catechisms, might rather — it may be thought — have repelled the youthful reader; and if these works did seem at times a little heavy, I could change them for the thundering sermons of Richard Cameron, the more glowing ones of James Renwick, or the weird, homely ones of Alexander Peden; or his " Prophecies" as told by Patrick Walker the peddler, which made my hair stand on end. Better than these, however, I had Baxter's " Saints Everlasting Rest" (a special favourite of my mother's), Halyburton's " Great Concern of Salvation," and Jonathan Edward's " History of the Work of Redemption"—works, these two last, of literary as well as doctrinal excellence. Then I had the fiery zeal of Boston's " Fourfold State." Also I had at hand Harvey's " Meditations among the Tombs," rather wordy and inflated I thought even then, and how the book came to be in my father's library I know not, for he declared that it was not free from Popery. The only poetry I had then within my reach was that contained in "Barrie's Collection," all of it excellent, however, and much of it quite classical, such as the noble "Elegy" of Gray and the beautiful episode of Lavinia in "The Seasons" of Thomson. The gloomy grandeur of Blair's "Grave" also impressed me greatly, and even at that early period the poetry of the Bible was my delight, and the Psalms particularly charmed me much, nor have they ceased to do so to this day.

By and bye I very early joined a library in Kilmarnock, the historical works of which I literally devoured, and likewise those of travel; indeed, at that time I read everything. I had no method in my reading, but just read whatever took my fancy. Those may speak against desultory reading who please, but my omnivorous and desultory reading has been in many ways the making of me, for I thus came to know somewhat of almost everything, which, had my reading been more methodical, I would not have done.

Very early too I began to write, not that I had at first any desire for authorship, but I wrote because when I found so many views and things in the world which I thought were wrong I could not help writing and saying so, and this has been the reason why for half a century I have hardly ever been out of one controversy or another. Latterly, however, my love of literature, and particularly of poetry, constrained me to write. My first published volume, as I have already stated, was one of very immature poetry, very *minor poetry* truly. It was published so long ago as the year 1846, and was dedicated to the then Earl of Eglinton and Winton, of illustrious and tournament fame, and who received the humble tribute most kindly, and its author also, who was sent for to Eglinton Castle by his Lordship, who received me in the frankest manner possible, and with whom I had a long talk, and left with a substantial proof of the good Earl's large heartedness.

Although the volume was far better received by the public than I had any right to expect, I published no more volumes—though I still continued to write for the newspaper press—for twenty years, though in 1874 I wrote a biographical sketch of John Johnston, the then still surviving veteran of Trafalgar—of whom I have already spoken—and edited his vigorous and meritorious poem entitled "Lord Nelson." In 1876, however, I published "Poems, Lectures, and Miscellanies," which was exceedingly well received by the press, the volume being now long out of print. Four years after, or in 1880, I published "The Circling Year and Other Poems," which was still better received by both press and public, and it also has long been out of print.

The great Covenanting struggle of the seventeenth century, and the gross injustice which these pious and devoted patriots, the Covenanters, had so long received—caused very much in the present age by the grossly unfair representations and caricaturing of them by Sir Walter Scott in his powerful and fascinating novel of "Old Mortality"—and my early knowledge of that appalling period of tyranny and persecution, with my frequent visits to their graves in the lonely moorlands, caused me, in 1886, to publish a volume on the Covenanters, entitled "Homes, Haunts, and Battlefields of the Covenanters." It was so well received that in 1888 I published a second volume, which was also exceedingly well received. Among those which cheered me most was a notice of it by the renowned Mr C. H. Spurgeon, in his "Sword and Trowel," in which, among other things, he said:—"We feel as much fascinated with these pages as in former days we were with Sir Walter Scott, but the charm is not that of a minstrel's words, but of holy fact and gracious truth. Oh for another twenty years of the Covenanters! This generation builds their sepulchres, but acts towards their testimony as their persecutors acted towards the men themselves. Mr Todd is a literary 'Old Mortality,' and diligently keeps alive memories of the brave men of God. Purchase and read his books and their influence will be salutary and strengthening." Mr Spurgeon also wrote me a private note, couched in equally kind terms. The public *did* purchase the volumes, but the bankruptcy of the publisher made the ready and large sale of no advantage to me. A second edition of the first series has been published by **R. W.** Hunter, 19 George IV. Bridge, Edinburgh, price 3s. 6d. The work has also been published in the United States of America. I have also a third series partly written, every volume being complete in itself.

Meantime, I had written a number of articles on the poets for *The Thistle*, an Ayrshire magazine, published by Mr Jones, Kilmarnock. In 1881 I wrote the sketches of Archibald M'Kay and J. K. Muir, both of Kilmarnock, and made the selections from their published volumes of poetry for the second volume of Edwards' "Modern Scottish Poets"; and for the following volume—Volume III.—I wrote no fewer than twenty-five of the biographical sketches, also making all the selections from their works, save one piece, for the sketch of Dr Walter C. Smith. Among my sketches in this volume are those of Thomas Aird, Miss M. P. Aird, Sarah Douglas Parker, Lady Flora Hastings, George Paulin, Wm. M'Dowall, John Wright, etc., etc. For Volume IV. I wrote three of the sketches, for Volume V. three, for Volume VI. six, and for Volume VII. five, and in all cases selecting the quotations—the whole from my pen being equal to one of the largest volumes of the series. I am the more particular in mentioning this because, though I have never been paid anything for my labours, not so much as my postages, save receiving the price (three shillings) of a single volume which I received to deliver to Lady Menteith of Mansfield, Mr Edwards would seem inclined to claim the credit of being the author of those sketches which are entirely from my pen, for in one of his prefatory notes, that to Volume VI., he flatteringly says:—"Mr A. B. Todd, the accomplished Ayrshire *literateur* and sweet and tender poet of Nature, to whom we have been indebted for much and valuable information in the course of our labours," etc. Had Mr Edwards said that I had done much of the work of these earlier volumes, he would only have stated the truth, and would not thus have been liable to mislead the reading public as to the authorship of a large number of the most important biographical sketches in these volumes.

The "Songs of the Covenant," mentioned by Professor Blackie in his letter quoted in the previous chapter, is a volume, the right title of which is "Poets and Poetry of the Covenant," with introduction by the Rev. David M'Allister, D.D., LL.D., of Alleghany, United States, America; and for which work I also wrote more than half of the biographical notices, and also made the quotations. That work was published in America, and likewise in this country by Mr R. W. Hunter, Edinburgh. Dr M'Allister (who is one of the most eloquent ministers and able writers of that great country), dedicated the volume to me in terms all too flattering. It was published so recently as 1894.

All throughout these years, I had many controversies in the city and provincial newspapers. I defended the poet Burns and Highland Mary from an unguarded attack of the Rev. Dr Wm. Hewison, of Rothesay, and did so successfully, according to excellent judges. I also smote the late Dr Charles Rogers, "hip and thigh," for his defence of the "Holy Willie" of Burns, and defeated both him and the late Dr Edgar of Mauchline, when they attempted to whitewash that dirty, canting creature, which all the waters of Damascus could not have made clean. Years and years ago I put the public right regarding what Burns meant when he sang about "Comin' through the Rye," though that *other Ishmaelite*, Mr Henley, is only said to have done so now! I have defended and fought long to prevent the gentle Michael Bruce from being robbed of the fame which is his righteous due as being the author of the "Ode to the Cuckoo" and other poems, and which by a few special and most illogical pleaders are being claimed for the immoral and wine-bibbing John Logan. I have had many a controversy regarding the Covenanters, and particularly in repelling the oft-refuted but always revived calumnies which have been brought against their memories, and whom again and again I have incontrovertibly proven to have been the noblest and most enlightened patriots of the age, and that they were the only opponents of a tyranny and a slavery under which all the wealthiest loyalists cringed, and have shown that what they fought for was civil and religious freedom, and that what they did in 1680 *the whole nation felt obliged to do in 1688*, when the Popish despot was driven from his throne, and the Revolution was brought about by the Covenanters at the cost of life itself, and that they secured for Britain those privileges which have secured for her the envy of the world.

In lesser matters I could not help taking up my pen and defending the good name and the honour of the wives of our Scottish peasantry and working men against an attack made upon them—thoughtlessly and inconsiderately and with no evil intention, I am sure—by the now Dowager-Marchioness of Bute, and in defence of these thrifty, worthy women I sent the following letter to *The Scotsman* newspaper, and as it will be a standing defence of the mothers, sisters, and wives of many of us at least, I give it here for preservation, I myself being peasant born and bred, I wrote as one of that class.

"LADY BUTE AND THE CONDITION OF THE LABOURING CLASSES IN SCOTLAND.

"SIR,—But for Lady Bute's high social position no attention whatever, I am certain, would have been paid by any one to what I am charitable enough to believe was the unintentional libel perpetrated by her the other day at Cardiff on this northern land from which she derives her title.

"From first to last Lady Bute—to use her own expression—manifests the most 'deplorable' ignorance of the habits, characteristics, and condition of the labouring classes of Scotland; for there never was a time, within the last fifty years at least, when the Scottish labourer made porridge the principal article of diet, although generally it was his meal once in the day. Neither is it the custom now for them to use tea with anything like the frequency stated by Lady Bute. And as for boiling tea in the morning and using that for all the other meals of the day, why, they will not use tea that has been boiled at all. That which they do use is infused in the ordinary way.

"It would be interesting to know how many Scottish labourers' cottages—not those merely born in Scotland, but of Scottish parentage—Lady Bute has ever visited. In any one of the four counties where her noble husband has a seat, and where they sometimes reside for a few days or weeks at a time, could she not count all the Scottish Protestant homes she has ever entered upon the fingers of her one hand? Lady Bute's mistake clearly is this—she has looked into a few of the cottages of her co-religionists, the Irish, whose habits of housekeeping are entirely different from those of the Scottish peasantry, and it is the picture of these, the very poorest and most ignorant natives of the Green Isle, which she depicts to the people of Cardiff as that of our thrifty, cleanly, tidy, and provident housewives. Of the habits and conditions of these 1 do not speak in ignorance, for I am not only a peasant-born Scot, but I have lived all my life among the labouring classes and common people. Forty years ago, I had occasion to be much in the island of Bute, and had not a little intercourse with the working classes there. I spent a summer in Galloway, in the near neighbourhood of Lord Bute's estate of Mochrum Castle. With the peasantry and labouring classes of Ayrshire few, if any, are more intimate, and for wellnigh half a century I have had my home in the valley of the Lugar, and almost within sight of Dumfries House. In all these places I have visited the homes and sat at the tables of many of the labouring classes, particularly in the great county of Ayr, from the lone Loch Maberry in the south, to the misty moors which lie around Lochgoin in the north, and from the bleak hills which rise above Glenbuck, and which hem in the green grave of the martyr of Priesthill in the east, to where 'the everlasting surges rave,' around the heads of Ayr in the west, and never once have I met with such a state of things as that described by Lady Bute in any of our genuine Scottish homes.

"Why does her Ladyship not advise a return to 'the nutritious porridge' instead of the use of vermicelli, that fushionless compound of flour, eggs, and saffron, or of maccaroni and such 'wheaten abominations,' as the great Christopher North used to call these, and the ''' . Oh!

K

for another such grand 'old man eloquent' to stand up for Scotland and her people, who in his review of the first edition of 'Stephen's Book of the Farm' offered this bet— He would take twenty Scottish ploughmen fed on oatmeal porridge and cakes, and allow the Cockney to take as many English ploughmen and feed them on any of their 'wheaten messes,' and the Scots, he said, would run, leap, wrestle, and fight the Englishmen, and would lick them to their hearts' content into the bargain. If I could, or dared to, lay a bet with Lady Bute, I would take as many Scottish boys, notwithstanding 'their deplorable physique,' and fed just as they are, and let her Ladyship bring as many of the same age from Cardiff or Cockneydom, as she pleases, and if the young Caledonians don't outrun the Southrons, make their ribs rattle on the ground, and paint their eyes black and blue and their noses red in less time than I take to write this, then I will never stand up for this 'land of the mountain and the flood' again.

"Truly the time has gone by when sneering at Scotland and her people in the heavy style of old Dr Johnson, or in the flippant manner of Charles Churchill—a rake, though a clergyman—who spoke of Scotland as a country 'where half-starved spiders feed on half-starved fleas,' will pass either for wit or for a truthful pourtrayal of the country or the people.

"I am sorry to have to write in this way of a lady who, by the hospital she has built and supports at Cumnock, and by many other kindly acts, has done so much to assuage the sufferings and the misery of mankind; but truth and patriotism compel me to speak thus plainly in defence of 'mine own, my native land,' of which the last of the great Border bards—the late Henry Scott Riddell—has thus so nobly and so truly sung—

> 'Ours is the land of gallant hearts,
>   The land of honoured graves,
> Whose wreath of fame shall ne'er depart
>   While proud the thistle waves.'

—I am, etc.   "AN AYRSHIRE PEASANT.
  "27th April, 1891."

In the midst of my many literary avocations a great
sorrow overtook me in the sudden death of my brother
William, who was three years my senior. The first
volume of my work on the Covenanters was then in pre-
paration, and in its progress he felt the most lively interest;
and in several of my pilgrimages to the martyrs' sepulchres
I was accompanied by him. I therefore miss him all the
more, and miss him still also because of his fine scholarship,
he having an excellent knowledge of Hebrew, Greek, and
Latin, which I have not, save only a little of the latter
language. He was one of the most warm-hearted, intelligent, and accomplished of men, and though twenty years
have glided by on the unstaying wings of time since he
passed away from earth to the better land, the unbidden
tears will yet at times dim my eyes ere I am aware, when
the memory of him and all he did and said wells up in my
breast. He died at Edinburgh on the 16th December,
1885, and in the *Cumnock Express* of the 26th of the same
month I thus conclude a lengthened poetical tribute to his
memory :—

> " Now thou with all life's ills hast parted,
> And I am left all broken hearted ;
> No more in summer I'll expect thee,
> No more thy wise words will direct me.
> Critic, thou wert severe yet kind,
> And never to my faults wert blind.
> Now mourns my muse thy cheering word,
> For that shall never more be heard ;
> And though I call, no answer ever
> Shall reach me over Lethe's river,
> Sure such fond ties were not in vain,
> And, sever'd, shall be knit again.
> Still nature prompts the falling tear
> For voice I never more shall hear,
> For form which ne'er shall meet mine eye,
> Till the last trump wails in the sky.
> Farewell ! Though still my bleeding heart
> From thoughts of thee can never part,
> Till I, like thee, shall pass away,
> And sleep forgotten in the clay."

CHAPTER XVI

CONCLUSION

> " Nor long the day
> Till we, like all, shall pass away !
> Yon sun that now our bosom warms
> Shall shine, but shine on other forms ;
> Yon grove whose choir so sweetly cheers
> Us now shall sound on other ears ;
> The joyous lamb, as now, shall play,
> But other eyes its sport survey ;
> The stream we love shall roll as fair,
> The flowery sweets, the trim parterre
> Shall scent, as now, the ambient air !
> The tree whose bending branches bear
> The one loved name shall yet be there,
> But where the hand that carved it ?   Where ? "
>
> INGOLDSBY LEGENDS.

LORD BYRON it is who says " Nothing so difficult as a beginning except perhaps the end."   The latter difficulty is the one which now perplexes me—how to begin the last chapter of this autobiography which has grown and expanded under my pen very much beyond what was either my intention or expectation.   It has been no ordinary pleasure to myself, however, to live, as it were in the writing of it, my life over again, and though my experiences in passing through that part of the vale of time which I have had to traverse may have been very much " the common lot " of most men of my station, still I may, I hope, have been able, by a faithful narration of the events, the ups and downs and the experiences of my life, to make the relation of some interest to others who are " sailing o'er life's solemn main "; and after a pretty lengthened and very varied experience indeed, I would give to those the excellent though rather stoical advice contained in these lines of " The Minstrel " of James Beattie, and by which I myself have been a good deal guided :—

148

" Of chance or change, O let no man complain,
    Else shall he never, never cease to wail;
For from the imperial dome, to where the swain
    Rears the lone cottage in the silent dale,
All feel th' assaults of Fortune's fickle gale."

In nothing which I have written have I hitherto said anything very definite regarding my religious beliefs, though it could very easily be inferred that in these I am both orthodox and unwavering. My firm belief in a God of providence as well as of grace, has kept me from sinking under many and great misfortunes and trials, and does so even now when old age is overtaking me and when, unlike the rich man in the parable, I have not " goods laid up for many years." But if—as I have often thought—the very birds of the air are under the Creator's care, how much more reason has man—the noblest of His works—to feel satisfied and convinced that He will care for him. Such our blessed Lord himself has made plain and placed beyond dispute in these words of His: " Behold the fowls of the air, for they sow not, neither do they reap, nor gather into barns; yet your Heavenly Father feedeth them. Are ye not much better than they? Consider the lilies of the field, how they grow; they toil not neither do they spin. And yet I say unto you, that Solomon in all his glory was not arrayed like one of these. If God so clothe the grass of the field, which to-day is and to-morrow is cast into the oven, shall He not much more clothe you, O ye of little faith?" We may have freewill in weaving the web of our lives, still all we do is under Divine control notwithstanding.

I grew up with a deep love for " the Book of Books "— the Bible—and no infidel books could ever in the least unsettle my firm, and I hope intelligent, belief in its truth; and I have read many such, though these I always found were passing down to oblivion one after another. On this very subject that great and eloquent speaker and writer, Edmund Burke, thus finely and truly says :—

" We have had writers of that description (infidels) who made some noise in their day. At present they repose in lasting oblivion. Who, born within the last forty years, has read one word of Toland, and Chub, and Morgan, and that whole race who called themselves Freethinkers? Who now reads Bolingbroke? Who ever read him through? Ask the booksellers of London what has become of all these lights of the world. In a few years they will go to the family vault of 'all the Capulets.' Because half a dozen grasshoppers under a fern make the field ring with their importunate chink, while thousands of great cattle, reposed beneath the shadow of the British oak, chew the cud and are silent, pray do not imagine that those who make the noise are the only inhabitants of the field; that, of course, they are many in number, or that, after all, they are other than the little, shrivelled, meagre, hopping, though loud and troublesome insects of the hour." Yes, and I, too, have seen a good many rise and make a noise, and who were going to do great things and reform the world by changing our belief in the Bible, or by abolishing it altogether. Where now is Bishop Colenso and his "Difficulties" regarding the Pentateuch? He is about as much forgotten and as little heard of and read as is now Lord Herbert of Cherbury, "The Father of English Deism." Who now hears of Bradlaugh, though but a few years dead? His works are as dead as his own *corpus*. The blatant Colonel Ingersol has followed the rest to the shades of oblivion, but the old Book remains unscathed, and it shall abide for ever. Not only were the laws of Nature to demolish much of what men were in the habit of believing, but we were being taught that such laws prevailed even in "The Spiritual World," and because of these "natural laws" we were, and are still being told, that we cannot therefore believe in the supernatural and miracles. I have thought that what that eminent French Protestant statesman and historian, Guizot, says on this subject in his "Meditations on Christianity," is not only excellent, but unanswerable— "True, general and constant laws do govern Nature. Are we therefore to affirm that these laws are necessary, and that no deviation from them is possible in Nature? Who is there that does not decern an essential, an absolute difference between what is general and what necessary?

The permanence of the actual laws of Nature is a fact established by experience, but it is not the only fact possible, the only fact conceivable by reason—those laws might have been other laws, they may change. Several have not always been what they now are; for science itself proves that the condition of the universe has been different from what it is at present; the universal and permanent order, of which we form part, and in which we confide, has not always been what we now see it; it has had a beginning; the creation of the actual system of Nature and of its laws is a fact as certain as the system itself is certain. And what is creation but a supernatural fact, and the act of a Power superior to the actual laws of Nature, and which has power to modify them just as much as it had power to establish them?"

These, in part, at least, are my scientific and philosophical reasons for believing in the revelation made to us in the Bible. I hope, however, that I have even a better foundation for my belief in Christianity —the "spiritual decerning" of the truth spoken of by St Paul in 1 Corinthians, chapter ii. Such passages of Scripture are "anchors of the soul," by which it may fix itself in a manner to outride every tempest of infidelity. By these the question of inspiration is settled in a word, so as to obviate the necessity, in spiritually-minded men, of giving themselves a moment's trouble about the voluminous impieties of the enemies of revelation.

To come back for a little, however, ere I close, to more worldly matters, and matters political and literary. In politics I have, from principle, been all my life a firm, conscientious, though moderate Conservative; and besides having been a voter of nearly sixty years' standing, I have always readily and vigorously employed my pen, both in prose and verse, in promoting the interests of my party, and as Othello said, I know that "I have done the State some service," and my party, in the county at least, know it too, and have long known it; and that at any moment, and on any phase of any political question, they could count upon my ready pen, and many trenchant articles. The other side were not slow at least to confess the damage I did to their candidates in times of contested elections. My party also know how they have rewarded me, during all these years, when my head has grown bald in their service. And should (as some day it must) my right hand lose its cunning, and my quick brain its power, and my ready pen can speed no more in the cause, and are at rest for ever, they may then miss and think of the old veteran who was never afraid to dash into the thickest of the fight.

It was to my action that the recent Edinburgh Burns forgeries of Howland Smith were detected. I received a letter from an Edinburgh gentleman of good position and excellent character, said to be one which had been written by Robert Burns, the poet, and also two poems. There was little in the letter, and the poems were poor enough, but the MSS. looked old, and the imitation of the handwriting of Burns being excellent, I published them in the *Cumnock Express* as a genuine letter and as genuine poems of Burns. This at once led to a controversy and a clever investigation by the *Edinburgh Evening Dispatch* as to the genuineness of the productions, and which led up to the detection of the system of fraud which had been going on for a length of time, and by which many men of skill—dealers in ancient MSS.—had been deceived. When after the most searching investigation I was unable to trace the " James Haig, Cumnock," to whom the letter was addressed, I joined the doubters, and soon the utter disbelievers in the genuineness of the MSS.

Two of the most remarkable events of my life have been my having occupied the chair at the celebration of the centenary of the birth of Robert Burns by the Cumnock Burns Club, and my occupying the chair again in the centenary year of his death, thirty-seven years after, and that too in the same place—the hall of the Dumfries Arms Hotel, Cumnock. On both occasions I proposed the memory of the poet, and as the circumstances are believed to be altogether unique in such celebrations, I have been urged to give the latter speech here, both for preservation, and also to show that my mental vigour had not in any way decayed, though that wide gulf of years lay between. Part

of what I said on the first occasion will be found in the
" Chronicle of the Hundredth Birthday of Robert Burns,"
collected and edited by the late Mr James Ballantine,
author of " Castles in the Air," etc., etc.—a work of
fully 600 large double-column pages, and containing a
record of 872 meetings.   In his account of the Cumnock
celebrations, the poet-editor characterised what I then
said on that occasion as " couched in glowing language."
The following, after a few introductory words, is what
I gave utterance to on 25th January 1896:—I now rise
to propose " The ever green, the immortal memory of
Robert Burns."   The present is no common anniversary
celebration, taking place as it does in the centenary year
of the poet's death ; for, as you are all aware, one hundred
years have all but passed away on the unwearied wings of
time since in that great brain of the bard " the worm alone
has been living where rapture had been."   To myself the
present celebration is one of great, peculiar, and possibly
also of unique interest ; for just thirty-seven years ago—
at the centenary celebration of the birth of Burns—I occupied
the same position as I do now, filled this same chair, in
this same hall, and proposed the same toast—the immortal
memory of Burns.   The intervening period from then till
now, is equal to the whole chequered lifetime of the poet,
save by a few months only.   What changes have taken
place in the world since then ! what changes in this company !   It moves me, gentlemen, too deeply for words to
express, to see here not one of all the seventy gentlemen
who were then present, and whom I then addressed !
Mostly those who composed that goodly company have
passed away from the walks of living men to the land of
deep forgetfulness ; and of the few who still remain, all,
I believe, have left the district and are now either tilling
the virgin soil of New Zealand, or are burning out life's
last embers beneath the scorching suns of Australia or
The Cape, or struggling with fate and fortune in the cold
dreary clime of Manitoba, while here I am left alone of all
that bright and enthusiastic company—left like a solitary
withering tree in a decaying forest !   It cheers me, however, to know—as I then predicted—that the fame of

Robert Burns is still widening and is becoming more universal as time continues its march, and that with us here, in Cumnock, the love and the reverence for the poet's memory are as great as ever, though from the altered constitution of our club now our numbers are not so large as they were thirty-seven years ago. If, therefore, it was true then, as I then said, that "like the circling and extending ripple which widens on the surface of a smooth lake when a stone is cast into its midst, his name and renown have extended until now that the splendour of his genius and the blaze of his fame have reached to earth's remotest bounds," much more certainly is this the case now, for wherever the British flag waves gloriously in the breeze of heaven, or the English tongue is spoken, the songs of this matchless bard of the people, of nature, and of humanity are heard. They awake the echoes which slumber on the banks of the Ganges, the Indus, the Murray, and the St Lawrence, or that sleep by "wild Ontario's boundless lake." They are chanted amid the far distant islands of "the melancholy main," and are sung all round the shores of Australia. And how is it that such is the case at this distant day nearly one hundred years after the large and warm heart of the bard had become cold in death, and is now but a clod of the valley? Other poets we have had, great masters of the poets' lyre, like Milton, who soared high up into the blue empyrean heaven of song; Shakespeare, who ranged all Nature through; Wordsworth, the great high priest of Nature; Scott, who revived the age of chivalry; Byron, who moved and thrilled every passion of the human soul; Hogg, the Ettrick Shepherd, who peopled the woods and desert wilds with beings not of earth, and pure and lovely as his own "Bonny Kilmaney's" self; Tennyson, whose poetry sounds "like music o'er a summer lake at the golden close of day," and many other bards, ancient and modern, who have sung nobly and well of love, friendship, patriotism, peace, and war, and of all that can move, agitate, or thrill the human soul; but not one of them has secured the same deep and abiding place in all hearts as Robert Burns, and this because of the universality of his genius, and his power to touch, to charm, to rouse, and to make all mankind nobler, better, and happier.   The most unlettered worker in factory or field hears in Burns the voice of a brother or a friend.   The artizan, amid the din of whirling wheels and the stunning clang of hammers, feels the hours pass pleasantly away while humming at his toil some one of the songs of glorious Robert Burns.   No less do they possess the power to please and to captivate high dames, noble earls, learned and grave philosophers, and all true and large-hearted preachers of righteousness.   Most other songs, however popular they may be for a season, have nearly all of them only their little day, and are forgotten.   But the songs of Burns—because they are fitted for all ages and for all ranks and conditions of men, and because they are so entirely true to Nature—are immortal.   It is these things, then, which, year after year, bring thousands of pilgrims from many a distant land to worship at the shrine of the rustic genius, and to gaze enraptured on the scenes which have been immortalised by his Muse.   On Cassills Dowans, still wearing its mantle of green, as when the poet, in imagination, saw the fairies blithely trip it there in the silvery light of the moon.   On " auld hermit Ayr," sweeping grandly by beneath the wood-crowned Braes of Ballochmyle and the red, beetling rocks, which lie between it and that other mansion of immortal song—the Castle of Montgomerie.   On the " Banks and Braes of Bonnie Doon," where the birds still sing as sweetly and merrily as when the large, lustrous eye of the poet glowed with rapturous delight to hear their notes ring along the glad, green banks of the ever-living stream.   The green braes of the pellucid Afton still attract the pilgrim's steps ; as do also the crimson-tippet daisies over yonder on the lea-rigs of Mossgiel, every rood and furrow of which have become hallowed ground from having been trod by the footsteps of " the bard who mourned the daisy's fate."   I will not attempt any critical analysis of the poems and songs of this greatest of the sons of men and the poet of all time.   This has been done again and again for a century by the most able of his biographers, from Dr Currie to Thomas Carlyle, and many times since the latter wrote his famous essay on the poet. The world has long felt their charm, and been influenced by their power. We all feel both to-night, and are convinced of their immortality.

> " Then pledge his mem'ry far and near, although the hand be
>   dust
>   That oft has swept the golden lyre that ages cannot rust ;
>   No sun of time ere sets upon the empire of his fame,
>   And all unwearied is the wing that bears abroad his name."

To your feet then, gentlemen, and drink with me, and with ringing cheers, " The Immortal Memory of Robert Burns."

Long, long before the bi-centenary of the birth of the poet comes round on the ever-revolving wheels of time, the hand that now traces these lines will have crumbled into dust, the quick brain of the writer will be still, and the form now so strong and vigorous will be but a clod of the valley ! Such has, however, been the lot of all mankind, since, in the lofty language of Milton :—

> " Man's first disobedience, and the fruit
>   Of that forbidden tree, whose mortal taste
>   Brought death into the world, and all our woe."

And the thought of it, to me at least, would be unbearable, were it not that the " Son of the Highest," as also " the Divine son of the most favoured of women " has, Himself, passed through and risen from the grave, and by His Gospel, and His own resurrection, " brought life and immortality to light." Therefore

> " 'Tis but a night, a long and moonless night ;
>   We make the grave our bed, and then are gone !
>   Thus at the shut of eve the weary bird
>   Leaves the wide air, and in some lonely brake
>   Cow'rs down, and doses till the dawn of day,
>   Then claps his well-fledg'd wings and bears away."

Few men, perhaps, have enjoyed more happiness in life than I, notwithstanding that for the last forty-three years, or since I was unexpectedly and harshly made to leave my tilework and farm on the Dumfries estate (getting not a penny of remuneration for the new machinery I had erected and the new tile kiln I had built at the one, or for the large amount of draining executed, and the new houses I had built at the latter), I have hardly ever been a month in advance of that want which, since then, has kept ever dogging at my heels. Hope, however, has always borne me up amid all my adversities and fears : and indeed I have always found with Sir Walter Scott :—

"That Hope is brightest when it dawns from fears."

Hope may "tell a flattering tale," still hope has been my anchor and my stay, and I at least could never say or sing with Miss Wrother in "The Universal Songster"—

"Hope tells a flattering tale,
     Delusive, vain, and hollow;
 Ah! let not Hope prevail
     Lest disappointment follow."

In 1903, however, on the occasion of my diamond jubilee as a journalist, I was very much cheered and honoured by some good friends getting up a testimonial to me, and presenting me with an address, and a handsome sum of money. The movement—I now know—was set agoing by one of the best men I have almost ever known —Mr William Anderson, wholesale stationer, Ingram Street, Glasgow. (See Appendix.) By the instrumentality also of some good and kind friends—all unknown to me— the Balfour Government, at that same time, conferred on me an annuity of forty pounds yearly ; so that in the opinion of some I am now—like Goldsmith's pastor of "The Deserted Village," "passing rich." I still, however, keep on editing, and writing largely for The Cumnock Express, and also writing much for The Ayr Observer. My salary is not large, but the work is congenial. Besides, I still find it necessary to do so ; and being blessed with good health, with my strength of body, my memory, and mental powers unimpaired by years ; thanks be to the God who has borne with me thus long, I am still as able as ever for the work.

And now, for the present, in bidding my readers farewell

I trust they have enjoyed part at least of the pleasure which it has given myself thus, as it were, to trace once more my many " wanderings through this world of care." And so I say in the words of Lord Byron—

> " Farewell! a word that must be and hath been,
>   A sound that makes us linger ; yet, farewell ! "

Yes, and linger I do, and I'm forced to say with that excellent man and pleasing poet—the late Dr David Macbeth Moir of Musselburgh—

> " Farewell !   There can be no farewell
>   To thee, loved, lost, langsyne ! "

APPENDIX No. I.

Mrs Agnes Drennen, or Kay, widow of James Kay, farmer, Sinclairston, in the parish of Ochiltree, who died in 1873 at the great age of 103 (I possess her memorial card), when as a girl served with John Rankine of Adamhill, when Burns, the Rev. John M'Math, assistant minister of Tarbolton, and other chosen friends of the witty farmer were frequent visitors there. She used to tell how that it had got noised abroad that on one occasion Mr M'Math, in company with Burns, had got intoxicated at Mr Rankine's house, and notice had been sent to him that the members of the Kirk Session were coming on a certain day to investigate the matter. Causing dinner to be prepared, he gave them a warm welcome on their arrival, and treated them to a glass of whisky till dinner was set. There being some little delay in this, they were induced to take another. They then had dinner. Mr Rankine having caused a kettle to be filled with whisky and used for warm water; after dinner, Mr Rankine said, "Now, gentlemen, we will have a glass of toddy and then to business." By this time they were all grown talkative, when Mr Rankine said, "Well, gentlemen, one glass more and then to business." Mr Rankine made the toddy, which, of course, was doubly strong, and as the glasses in which he dealt it round to the elders were large, by this time they had forgot all about the "business," and in a little while they were all so drunk that not one of them could walk; and it being summer and the sun still shining in the heavens, Mr Rankine caused his man to yoke a long-body, or hay-cart, into which they were all got huddled and driven home, and let off at their several doors in the village reeling drunk, to the consternation of the villagers; when nothing more was heard— in the Session at least—of the *bouze* of the Rev. Mr M'Math and Burns. Mrs Kay was a woman of the highest character, and the amusing trick played on the elders by the " rough, rude, ready-witted Rankine," may be fully relied upon in all its particulars.

No. II.

Extract from the Kilmarnock Standard, 10*th October* 1903.

ON Saturday afternoon, 3rd October 1903, in the Dumfries Arms Hotel, Cumnock, Mr A. B. Todd was entertained to luncheon on the occasion of the celebration of his diamond jubilee as a journalist. He was at the same time presented with an illuminated address and a cheque for £168, 15s. The chair was occupied by Mr Wm. Wallace, LL.D., of the *Glasgow Herald*, with Mr Arch. Brackenridge, town clerk of Cumnock, acting as croupier. There were also present:—Mr Wm. Anderson, Glasgow, hon. secretary of the movement; Mr David Fortune, J.P., Glasgow; Mr Robert Braid, J.P., Glasgow; Bailie Graham, D.L., Glasgow; Mr George Dunlop, *Kilmarnock Standard*; ex-Provost Ferguson, *Ayr Observer*; Mr George M'Millan, publisher of the *Cumnock Express*, and others. After a splendid luncheon had been partaken of, the Chairman gave the loyal toasts, which were pledged with all enthusiasm.

Mr Anderson, in making the presentation, said:—Mr Todd, the Address which I have now the honour of placing in your hands on this most important occasion is as follows:—

"To Mr A. B. TODD,

Editor of The Cumnock Express, *Author of ' The Circling Year,'*
' Homes, Haunts, and Battlefields of the Covenanters,' etc.

"DEAR SIR,

        The undersigned, in the name of many of your friends in the West of Scotland, would desire to tender to you our heartiest congratulations upon your having entered upon your sixtieth year as a contributor to the Press, your first communication having been made to the *Kilmarnock Journal* in May 1844.

"A Diamond Jubilee in Journalism is an event of extreme rarity, and its occurrence will naturally call to your mind the many changes that have taken place in the field of literature during these sixty years—the abolition of the Advertisement duty and of the Stamp and of Paper duties, which have so completely revolutionised the Newspaper Press, that instead of the daily and weekly newspapers being the luxury of the few, they now find their way into almost every house in the Kingdom.

"It has been your privilege to render good service in defending the "Cause of the Covenant," and to take a prominent part in the erection of Memorials to Peden at Cumnock, Howie at

Lochgoin, Hyslop at Sanquhar, Pollok at Mearns, and the recently erected Memorial at Bothwell Bridge.

"As a lifelong admirer of Robert Burns, our National Poet, you have had the unique experience of presiding at Cumnock at the centenary gathering in January 1859, and again at the subsequent gathering held at the same place thirty-seven years thereafter in 1896.

"In thus handing to you a tangible, if slight, expression of our respect, we note with pleasure that your services to literature have been recognised by an annuity from the Royal Bounty Fund. It is our earnest desire that you may be spared for many years to enjoy it, and that in a green old age you may continue by word and pen those labours with which your name has been associated during your long and busy life.

"In name of the Committee,

"ARCH. BRACKENRIDGE, *Hon. Treasurer.*
"WM. ANDERSON, *Hon. Secretary.*

"CUMNOCK, *3rd October* 1903."

And now, my dear sir, in asking your acceptance of it, allow me to state that I feel it to be no small honour to have had, along with other willing workers, some hand in bringing to a successful issue this tangible expression of the respect in which you are held by many friends scattered over the kingdom, but more especially in the West of Scotland, and I am sure that it is the earnest desire of all interested that you may be long spared to go out and in amongst us; aye, and even yet, should occasion require it, to "buckle on your armour" by word or pen in defence of the "Cause of the Covenant" as of yore. Mr Chairman and gentlemen, I daresay you will bear with me when for a few minutes I refer to my acquaintanceship with our good friend Mr Todd, and how in more than one undertaking we have been associated together. We met in spirit in the correspondence columns of the *Glasgow Herald* some years before we saw each other in person —many meet there who never see each other face to face. Some years thereafter, when I endeavoured to take the place of an old friend now gone in the matter of the centenary of James Hyslop, the gifted author of "The Cameronian Dream," the first man to lend me real assistance was Mr Todd. Other willing helpers soon joined us, and through the united efforts of those interested, a handsome monument stands on the banks of the Crawick within

L

easy distance of the historic burgh of Sanquhar. The same may be said of joint interest taken in the matter of the centenary monument to Robert Pollok, of "Course of Time" fame, at Newton Mearns. In my intercourse with Mr Todd, I soon found that he was one of those 'sparce' men who possess the power of raising you above an everyday platform, more particularly did I feel this in listening to his speech as chairman at a gathering of the natives of Cumnock held in Glasgow some years ago, his subject being the "Psalms of David and the Songs of Burns." The psalms touched the spiritual nature of man, and led him to trust and reverence the great Creator, and the truly national songs of Robert Burns, gave him a spirit of manly independence, of which, as a nation, we have no cause to feel ashamed. Judging from what I have read, I would say if there was any place where our good friend excelled, it was when presiding at a Burns gathering on the 25th January—this hotel, possibly this very room, is the scene of one of his early triumphs. This in more than one quarter has been repeated, the true spirit of poesy possessed by himself enabled him to attain a height reached only by a few, yet "at that height he felt himself at home." (Applause.)

Mr Brackenridge said—I am sure it is exceedingly gratifying to the committee in charge of the testimonial to our friend Mr Todd that, through the kindness of his numerous admirers, they are enabled to supplement the presentation of the beautiful address, which the honorary secretary, Mr Anderson, has just so ably performed, by offering Mr Todd something further, and of a more useful description. In response to the appeal of the committee, it was my pleasing duty, as honorary treasurer, to receive and acknowledge something like 200 contributions, and that from all ranks and conditions of men, both at home and abroad. While it was very satisfactory, indeed, to receive so many subscriptions, our friend Mr Todd will no doubt appreciate that the value of these monetary acknowledgments is greatly enhanced by the many kind letters which accompanied the enclosures, all testifying in high terms to his literary abilities, and wishing the movement every success. I may be permitted to add that a considerable number of these correspondents stated that they had only the pleasure of knowing Mr Todd through the medium of his graphic pen. As honorary treasurer I beg to report that the total contributions received, with a small amount of bank interest accrued thereon, amount to £177, 1s. 1d., from which there fall to be deducted for outlays, including the cost of the address, printing, postages, etc., a sum of £8, 5s. 7d., leaving a net sum in my hands of £168, 15s. 6d. And now, Mr Todd, in name of the contributors and on behalf of the committee, I have the honour to ask your acceptance of this cheque for £168, 15s. 6d., and I do so with the sincere hope that in good health and happiness you may be spared to enjoy a well earned-rest. (Applause.)

Mr Anderson at this stage said he had to intimate several apologies for absence. He had seen Lord Overtoun personally, and his lordship had expressed his deep regret at not being able to be present that day, but not content with that his lordship had sent a kindly letter, in which he had repeated his regret and expressing his great satisfaction that the movement had been so successful. The Rev. Dr Kerr, of the Reformed Presbyterian Church of Glasgow, had also written expressing regret, and hoping that that day's function would be successful. The Rev. John Brown, of Paisley, and Mr Robert Ford had written in similar terms, and both of them desired that their warm respects be conveyed to Mr Todd. (Applause.)

The Chairman then proposed the toast of the day, "Our Guest—Mr Todd." Dr Wallace said the greater part of his duty had been taken out of his hands by the sympathetic references that had just been made to Mr Todd by Mr Anderson and by Mr Brackenridge. They had fully given expression to the sentiments they all held regarding their guest. (Applause.) As a matter of fact, he (Dr Wallace) did not know why he should have been honoured in being asked to preside over that meeting except for two reasons which presented themselves to his mind. The first was that he was connected with the newspaper Press, though he had not been connected with it for the long period of sixty years —still there was no saying what he might accomplish seeing the inducements which were being held out that day. (Laughter and applause.) The other reason was his personal appreciation of the valiant way Mr Todd had, from his youth to his green old age, conscientiously striven for what he believed to be the right. He was a worthy veteran who had always said what was in his mind, and he had said it in no uncertain way. (Applause.) After making jocular references to Mr Todd's style in controversy and associating this with Breezyhill, Dr Wallace went on to say that their friend had written much about their Covenanting forefathers and about Burns, and they had great reason to be proud of the fact that he recognised that the spirit of the one animated the spirit of the other. The Doctor, in a few words, described Burn's attitude to the Covenant, and quoted with singular effect one or two

poems he had seen on this point.   There was no denying the fact
that the doings of the Covenanters sometimes brought a smile and
sometimes a tear, but at the same time all who understood the covenanting cause knew that it was fundamentally right.   (Applause.)
It was greatly to the credit of Mr Todd that in all his writings he
had tried to show the truth of these points which they all at the
present day so much desired.   (Applause.)   The Chairman had
the greatest satisfaction in taking part in the movement to honour
Mr Todd, because he had sprung from the ranks of the people—
he belonged to the moral aristocracy of Scotland, to the people
who had faced the realities of life, and who had solved the prob-
lems of existence and religion for themselves.   (Loud applause.)
Mr Todd had lived a strenuous life until now, he had reached a
green old age—in fact, he was not old at all, for he was with them
that day full of strength and vigour, and their sincere hope was
that he might long continue to enjoy the respect and confidence of
his friends.   Dr Wallace then in graceful terms asked the company to pledge the very good health of their friend.

The toast having been responded to with the utmost enthusiasm,
another cheer, on the happy suggestion of the Chairman, was given
for the good wife of their guest.

Mr Todd, on rising, said — Mr Chairman and gentlemen, after
listening to the exceedingly kind things which I have just heard
said of myself, and after receiving such a beautiful and, I fear,
much too laudatory address, I cannot help asking myself if, really,
I am deserving of it all, and of such a magnificent testimonial,
contributed to by friends in all parts of the kingdom, and by some
even in other lands who know me only by name.   I am therefore
at a loss for language in which I may sufficiently express my
thanks, my deepest gratitude for it all.   Sprung from a long line
of Scottish peasant farmers, I owe nothing to position, to inherited
wealth, or even to education, beyond what, in my young days, was
imparted by the learned and diligent parish and other school-
masters of the later twenties and the early thirties of last century.
Whatever literary taste and talent I have I owe in a great measure
to an excellent, pious, and noble-minded mother, possessed as she
was of a great love for and knowledge of the ancient ballad lore and
the gems of our Scottish song-literature.   My excellent father,
again, early made me acquainted with the history of the great
Covenanting struggle for civil and religious liberty in Scotland ;
and from him I learned to admire the noble men and women who,
under the two last Stuart kings, were persecuted to the death
(many of them at least) "for righteousness sake," and of

whose callous and cruel persecutors, I would say with the poet :—

> " Tyrants ! could not misfortune teach,
> That man has rights beyond your reach ?
> Thought ye the torture and the stake
> Could that intrepid spirit break,
> Which even in woman's breast withstood
> The terrors of the fire and flood ? "

Constant readers of our grand old English Bible, my excellent parents made me early acquainted with it too, and from my mother —whose memory is very dear to me still—I inherited an intense love for, and admiration of, its poetic books, whether " the rapt Isaiah " sang of the future glories of the millennial day, or the patriarch Job and his friend wrestled with the mysteries of life, or " the sweet singer of Israel " tuned his harp upon the lovely heights of Mount Zion, or when the beloved disciple, John, in part at least, withdraws the veil which conceals the unspeakable glories of the New Jerusalem. Nor has my early love for the poetry of the Bible, or for poetry in general, in the least decreased, now that I am past the far fourscore. To my dear departed mother, however, and to the Bible, which she so much loved, I owe more—even in a literary point of view—than to all else in the world beside. In making myself well acquainted with the scenes and sufferings of the heroic Covenanters of the seventeenth century, I have read much and travelled far and frequently, and, as you know, have written a good deal ; and it is impossible for me to describe my feelings when, often far out and all alone in the desert wilds, I stood by the lonely grave of some one who had had a burial of blood in the dark days of the Covenant times :—

> " The mossy pass, the mountain flood,
> Still hallowed by the patriot's blood ;
> The rocky cavern, once his tent,
> And now his deathless monument,
> Rehearsing to the kindling thought
> What faith inspired and valour wrought."

Robert Burns has told us that the Muse found him at the plough, but she found me earlier in life and at a much more lowly occupation still ; she found me herding cows by the green burnsides in the parish of Sorn (although later in life I have held the plough, too) and among the lonely moors of Fenwick (my father's native parish, and which, because of William Guthrie, its first and its Covenanting minister, and the famous Howies of Lochgoin, was to him the

Holy Land). Had you seen me among these moors then, gentle-men, barefoot and with my dog and my plaid, or sometimes, instead of a plaid, with a goatskin tied round my shoulders as a protection from the rain on those misty moors, you would have thought me much more likely to frighten than to allure the nymphs of Parnassus; and yet my rough and primitive dress did nothing of the kind, for from an eminence on the farm I had views of what tended to inspire both my patriotism and my poetic fancy. My patriotism, for away up in the east was Lochgoin with its many thrilling Covenanting memories, and from which lonely moorland solitude, for so many centuries, daily praise and prayer had ascended right up into the listening ear of Jehovah. Of poetry, for far away down in the west, on a clear day, I could see the glittering and gleaming waters of the Firth of Clyde, with the great ships continually coming and going, and with the lofty and splintered peaks of Arran, "robed by distance in an azure hue," or bathed in floods of rosy, crimson, or saffron light, as the great flaming sun dipped behind the rocky pinnacles of Goatfell! Poetry, to me, like Coleridge, "has been its own exceeding great reward," and as I grew up I became acquainted with and revelled in the works of Shakespeare, Spenser, Milton, Dryden, Pope, Young, Gray, Goldsmith, Blair, Beattie, Burns, Scott, Byron, Hogg, Pollok, and many others, and in whose works I revel still. It was at my mother's knee, however, that I first became charmed by poetry, as she would recite to me some of our grand old national ballads, or in a voice of seraphic sweetness she would sing to me "The Soldier's Return" of Burns or "The Wounded Hussar" of Campbell. To her fine example, literary taste, and winning Christian ways I owe anything that is good in me; and even yet, although she has now been more than forty years in the better land, the remembrance of her still greatly influences my life, and I feel as if her gentle spirit was daily luring me on to the Beulah which is above. I have had both the smiles of Fortune and its frowns in my pretty long journey through life. But of this I will not now speak. Having always been connected with one news-paper or another for more than fifty-nine years now, and with the *Cumnock Express* and *Ayr Observer* for exactly thirty-three years of that period, I have taken part in many controversies, religious, literary, and political; yet this I will say, never once, in all these years, have I advocated what I did not *believe* to be right; and although I have both got and given many pretty hard raps; yet do I believe that I have never been at all hated by any of my opponents, and I can freely say that I have never borne any ill-will to any one of them all, however much I may have disliked many of their ways and opinions. The Government, as you know, has been kind to me, although, right or wrong, I have been of no little service to my party too; far more so, I am certain, than those in high places are aware of. Your kindness, however, and that of the many subscribers to this magnificent testimonial, I value most; and if I only mention the names of two gentlemen connected with the testimonial—those of the exceedingly energetic and courteous honorary secretary, Mr William Anderson, and Mr Archibald Brackenridge, the kind and genial treasurer, and—shall I say it?— the prudent banker and upright lawyer, it is not because I do not greatly appreciate the kindness and aid of every member of Committee, and of all the subscribers. To the press, also, I owe my warmest thanks, for without an exception it has spoken most kindly of me at this time. Years, doubtless, now are beginning to multiply upon my head, but thanks to a gracious Providence they still sit lightly there; and with memory still unimpaired my poetic sympathies as keen, and my interest in passing events as great, as they were fifty years ago, I hope yet to do some good journalistic and literary work; and thanking you all, gentlemen, and all my friends, the subscribers, with all my heart, and much more so than I can express, and Dr Wallace very especially for his great and greatly appreciated kindness in coming south to preside at this meeting; I resume my seat with a repeated expression of warmest thanks. (Applause.)

Mr D. Fortune proposed "The Press." It was, he said, a toast which could not fail to meet with acceptance from the company gathered round that table. They were presided over by a distinguished *litterateur* in the person of Dr Wallace, who was adorning his present position as he had adorned every position he held. (Applause.) Then they were met to do honour to the grand old man of journalism, whose pen had ever been associated with all that was good, pure, and honourable. Then again they had with them such well-known newspaper men as Mr Dunlop of the *Kilmarnock Standard* and Mr Ferguson of the *Ayr Observer*, two of their best known and most ably conducted county newspapers. (Applause.) For these reasons Mr Fortune was sure that his toast would be received with appreciation. (Applause.) He claimed to have a personal knowledge of newspaper work, and a fairly wide acquaintance with the newspaper press as a whole, and he could give it as his conviction that for purity of purpose, appreciation of honest effort, for elevation of thought, for the high tone of its morality, and for the all-round ability with which it was conducted, the Scottish Press was without an equal in the world. (Applause). It would be impossible with the time at his disposal to deal with all that the Press of the country had done for the people. The time was when it was called the Fourth Estate—the time had come when it must be called the First Estate. (Applause.) After a passing allusion to the Fiscal Policy, and to the fact that none of us would have known anything about it but for the Press, Mr Fortune made special reference to the newspapers of the West of Scotland. He had been directly associated with many public movements, and there was especially one to which he would like to refer—namely, that in connection with the Royal Infirmary. The Press of Glasgow had given him ungrudging assistance—assistance which could not possibly be bought with money. (Applause.) He had been greatly pleased to be associated with the movement which was so happily culminating that day, and he sincerely wished that their guest might long be spared to wield his facile pen. He was happy to meet such able editors as Mr Dunlop and Mr Ferguson, with whose names he had pleasure in coupling the toast. (Applause.)

Mr Dunlop said, in reply, he had to thank Mr Fortune for the generous way in which he had referred to the newspaper press as a whole, and to that portion of it which was identified with the West of Scotland. He was pleased to be present that day to do honour to his friend Mr Todd. It was many years since Mr Todd had first contributed to the *Standard*, and he (Mr Dunlop) was pleased to think that it was in the columns of the *Standard* that their guest's autobiography had appeared in a series of deeply interesting articles. Many friends were waiting for the publication of this autobiography, and he hoped it would not be long delayed. (Applause.) Speaking for his own newspaper, Mr Dunlop could say that the work of no contributor was read with greater pleasure than were the writings of Mr Todd. He wished to join in all the good wishes that had been so eloquently expressed by the previous speakers. (Applause.)

Mr Ferguson, in a few appropriate words, referred to his long and intimate association with Mr Todd. Their friendship had necessarily been of the closest kind, and the harmony had been perfect. He cordially endorsed all that had been said by all who had already spoken. (Applause.)

Bailie Grahame proposed "The Committee," and in the course of his remarks said that forty-six years ago he had been connected with the Press in sending paragraphs about the abnormal gooseberry, etc., from Beith to the *Ardrossan Herald*. He had discovered that there was more money in selling the paper after it had been soiled with printer's ink than there was in selling it fresh from the hands of men like his friend Mr Anderson. (Laughter.) In a happy way Bailie Grahame claimed to be a very important personage in the newspaper world, for what would be the use of newspapers if there was no one to distribute them. In coming back to his toast, he had to warmly congratulate the Committee upon the excellent results of their labours, and he also added a word of kindly regard for Mr Todd.

Messrs Anderson and Brackenridge made most appropriate replies.

Mr Braid proposed "The Chairman." They were all delighted—they were indeed much honoured—in having Dr Wallace to preside over their little gathering. The Doctor by his genius had won a lasting fame in the literature of Scotland, and they had all been greatly pleased that he had been able to spend the day with them in doing honour to a distinguished brother of the pen. (Applause.) He was glad to hear that Mr Todd had sprung from a race of peasants. Our ablest men had risen from lowly surroundings. Mr Braid then, in singularly appropriate terms, proposed the toast which stood in his name, and Dr Wallace made a felicitous reply.

The singing of " Auld Lang Syne " brought the proceedings to a close. Later in the afternoon the company visited Mr Todd's home, Breezyhill, where Mrs Todd entertained her visitors to a good old-fashioned Scotch tea. This after-meeting was also greatly enjoyed.